Ex Libris

Peter Mudgett
christmas 1990
from Dom.

Living at the End of Time

John Hanson Mitchell

Other Books by John Hanson Mitchell

THE CURIOUS NATURALIST

CEREMONIAL TIME

A FIELD GUIDE TO YOUR
OWN BACK YARD

LIVING AT
THE END OF TIME

John Hanson Mitchell

HOUGHTON MIFFLIN COMPANY BOSTON 1990

For information about permission to reproduce selections from
this book, write to Permissions, Houghton Mifflin Company,
2 Park Street, Boston, Massachusetts 02108.

Library of Congress Cataloging-in-Publication Data

Mitchell, John Hanson.
Living at the end of time / John Hanson Mitchell.
     p.   cm.
     ISBN 0-395-44594-9
    1. Mitchell, John Hanson.   2. Naturalists — United States —
Biography.   I. Title.
QH31.M52A3   1990
508'.092 — dc20 89-48549
[B] CIP

Printed in the United States of America

FFG 10 9 8 7 6 5 4 3 2 1

The ornaments used in this book are taken from Andrew
Jackson Downing's *A Treatise on the Theory and Practice
of Landscape Gardening,* published in 1841. Courtesy
of the Boston Athenaeum.

For my mother

Contents

Author's Note

The events described in this book occurred in what we in the West, by collective agreement, refer to as the past. I have a good memory for past events, but I do not accept entirely the normal constraints of time and space. The past is an ill-perceived, even controversial state, and it is not necessarily compatible with absolute truth — if there is such a thing. So if I got things mixed up in this book, if I have somehow seen, in an otherwise unremarkable landscape, a mystic forest in which bears and Indians and events long past seem to coexist with industrial parks and superhighways, then I say blame the confusion of time. I am only setting down here what I perceived to be true during the year in which I lived in that forest, successfully disguised to the world as a normal twentieth-century man.

Having said that, I want to take this opportunity to either thank or apologize to a number of people involved in the production of this book. I am grateful to the people at the Thoreau Lyceum in Concord for their help in the preparation of the Thoreau material, in particular Anne McGrath and her staff. And I would especially like to thank Thomas Blanding and Edmund A. Schofield for reading and correcting parts of the manuscript. I am also grateful to Brenda Palmucci for her laborious typing, Harry Foster for his laborious editing, and, finally, William Reiss for his constant endurance.

Certain friends, allies, and acquaintances helped with the construction of my cottage and lent certain hand tools, which I hope I have returned in reasonably good condition.

Finally, I want to apologize to those who appear in this account for any liberties, intentional or unintentional, that I may have taken with the stories of their lives. Those who still count themselves among the living will know what I mean; the others probably won't care.

Living at the End of Time

1 Uncommon Ground

JUST TO THE EAST of Beaver Brook, in an area known to geologists as the Schooly Penaplain, there is a low ridge that rises from the swampy shores of a small lake and runs south-southeast for half a mile or so. Coming on that place from any of the four quarters of the globe, you would not say that it was in any way unique. To the east, a patchwork of overgrown hay fields rolls up from the flood plain of the brook; to the west and south, sheep pastures, hay fields, and plots of vegetables rise to the forested higher ground; and on the north you can see a dark woods of oak and pine and hemlock. Except for the fact that the aspect of the place is generally rural and pleasing to the eye, the area is not unlike a thousand similar ridges that interlace the coastal plain of New England.

I once spent a year living in a small cottage I built on the eastern slope of that ridge. The place was hardly new territory for me; I had already lived on the hill for some fifteen years before I built my small house. But the more I got to know the land in that area, the more I walked the woods and the edges of the fields, the more the ridge drew me in. The place became a center for me, the very core of my personal universe; it seemed impossible for me to live a full life anywhere else. The world was unbounded there, as if all experience, all history, had some-how concentrated itself in this singular spot. I was forever stumbling on new adventures, new landscapes, and improbable occurrences. The ridge invited improbability.

In the woods behind my cottage the land broke into a series of small, angled valleys and deep hollows. Here, a century ago, there were three or four farms, and in the deeper woods I would find sad little remembrances of past lives — dooryard lilacs, beds of daffodils, irises, and lonely stands of poppies and peonies. I discovered running walls, old foundations, the skeletons of cars and farm wagons and hay rakes. There were owls and coyotes, foxes and eagles and hawks, and it seemed to me that even wilder things could be found if one bothered to look — fishers, bobcats, bears, perhaps even Indians. It was a haunted land, deserted now, unlived in, unloved, untracked, and as yet undiscovered by the working population of the community in which the ridge was located.

I used to have experiences in that forest that did not make sense, that didn't mesh with our vision of the way the world is supposed to operate here in the rational, scientific West. Inside the depths of the woods things seemed to change overnight. An old wagon road at the bottom of the ridge, deserted since 1893, would alter its course of its own volition. A huge oak tree near the road would shift periodically and reappear somewhere else. There was an Indian burial ground among some boulders on the western slope of the ridge; people used to say that well into this century Pawtucket Indians could be seen in that part of the woods. The ghost of a soldier, slain in King Philip's War in 1676, used to appear on the ridge. Once, a hundred and fifty years ago, the last bear in the region was killed in a hemlock grove on the north slope, not far from my cottage. It was said that after it died, it came to life again and, just before it expired for the second time, turned itself into an Indian.

I never knew who I would meet in the woods. Once, years ago, I encountered a man there who dressed in the skins and furs of wild animals and claimed to subsist by hunting and gathering. I would occasionally see a family of serious-looking people dressed in corduroy, picking mushrooms in the woods. They turned out to be Eastern Europeans, immigrants who maintained a self-sufficient small farm in a four-acre clearing just south of the lake. Nearby lived a woman who would always dress impeccably to do her gardening work and spoke with a clipped Anglo-American accent. Her land was a veritable Eden of blossoming flowers, trees, and shrubs; it used to be said in the town that she had the ability to make plants flourish by simply staring at them. Occasionally I would see her in the woods as well, always under unusual circumstances.

One afternoon in September I was crossing a meadow just below the hickory grove where I eventually built my cottage when I heard a tiny bell ring out from the grasses beside one of the stone walls that interlace the ridge. I listened for a second or two and then realized that the bell was nothing more than the singing of a meadow cricket, not an uncommon sound in September in this part of the world. But as I stood there, I noticed that other crickets were calling in the meadow, and that they were singing with far more intensity than they normally would do. The volume increased until the sound was almost deafening; the high, insistent ringing filled the space above the grasses; it shimmered in the upper air; it surged against the wall of woods beyond the stone walls and rolled back on itself. Crickets were everywhere; I had never heard such wild singing. And then, in the midst of this frenetic calling, the sun flashed and the forest wall turned an impenetrable black. I had a sense that something momentous was about to happen. The inner nature of the ridge, the nature of reality, perhaps, was about to reveal itself to me. In the dark interior of the woods I could see moving shapes. Birds flew past. Branches swayed in spite of the stillness, and I thought I saw something large rise up from behind the stone wall and lumber off into the obscurity of the deeper woods.

I went after it. I crossed the wall and walked a few yards into the trees; but as soon as I stepped into the shaded interior, the crickets in the meadow behind me fell silent. A long corridor of flat ground opened in front of me, carpeted with partridgeberry and mayflower, and at the end of the hall of trees I saw the figure of a woman in a print dress holding a white rabbit in her arms. She appeared to be fifty-five or sixty, and had her gray hair tied in a bun at the back of her neck. She turned and looked at me directly. Then she gathered her rabbit closer to her and walked away.

Or was that part of a dream I had? I was forever dreaming about the place, and sometimes I couldn't be sure what was dream and what was real. I knew this woman — she was the gardener who lived on the other side of the ridge who could make things grow by staring at them. In a more rational world, or in a more rational place, she would have spoken to me. But then the ridge was out of step with time.

I did not set out to explore the mysteries of the place the year I lived there. What I really wanted to do was think. My wife and I had separated a year before I built my cottage, and for a while I had rented an apartment about three miles from the ridge. But life was dull there. I sometimes felt drained and unconnected. I would go back to the ridge and walk around, and I would always come away with a sense of energy and renewal. The place had power; there was something about it that nourished me. At the end of the year I decided to return and build a cottage in the woods, behind my old house. I could be closer to my two children by living on the ridge. I could be closer to the mysterious wooded slopes. Set back from lights and roads and noise, I could attain that singular state that is so hard to find in our time — solitude.

This move was not a new development in my life. From an early age I had planned to retire at twenty-seven to a small country village, there to watch the passage of the seasons and study the smaller details of life — the frogs and the crickets, the flights of migratory birds, and the blossoming of the forest. I took as my model for this the champions of the small life, Gilbert White in Selbourne, England, and closer to home, Henry Thoreau, who spent two years living by the side of Walden Pond in Concord, far enough from civilization to experience the adventure of living close to the natural world, but not so far away that he couldn't walk home for dinner.

In some ways I had already achieved my goal. At age twenty-seven I had left New York City and had taken a job teaching little children about nature in a small town in northwestern Connecticut. After that I lived in Europe for a while, then on Martha's Vineyard, and then I moved to the valley with the low ridge. These were all pleasant enough years, but there always seemed to be too many windows and walls between me and the natural world. What I needed, what I had always wanted, was a one-room cabin where I could wake up and step outside without getting dressed.

Once I had decided to build, I spent a lot of time on the back lot trying to choose the best possible place to site my cottage. I finally settled on a spot just beyond a small meadow, in the copse of young hickory trees, not far from the hemlock grove where the last bear in the valley was killed in 1811. The site had southern exposure, good winter sun, dappled shade in summer, and the bright, flowery expanse of the meadow to the southeast.

No one in the United States who decides to spend a year or so living in a cabin in the woods, watching the course of the seasons, does so without at least a nod to Henry Thoreau, and this experiment was to take place in the heart of Thoreau country, no more than sixteen miles from Walden Pond. I was working in Lincoln, Massachusetts, two miles from the site of Thoreau's cabin, and regularly on clear days I would walk there. After a few years, almost in spite of myself, Henry began to insinuate himself into my life. One hundred and thirty years after his death he still had a presence in the area; I could not walk anywhere near Walden Pond without thinking about him. I began to read his works. I studied *Walden;* I read *A Week on the Concord and Merrimack Rivers,* and I delved into some of the editions of his journals. When I went to construct my small house, quite logically, I considered building a version of Henry's cabin at Walden.

It seemed a propitious time to undertake such a project. Down at the Walden Pond Reservation the state government was in the process of constructing an exact replica of the cabin. I knew Roland Robbins, the man who had discovered the actual site of the cabin, and who was overseeing the construction of the replica. Robbins gave me a set of plans for Henry's cabin and encouraged me to use them. But studying the spare, hard lines, I began to wonder whether I really wanted such a place. My tastes in architecture (not to mention world views) differed from Henry's. The cloistered, spartan life led by Thoreau, while attractive in a theoretical way, did not quite match my semicivilized style. Furthermore, I had to face certain significant realities. Thoreau went to the woods because he wished to live deliberately and confront only the essential things in life. I went there because my wife and I had separated and the woods were the only place I could find affordable housing.

In addition to Thoreau's works, I had been reading those of Andrew Jackson Downing, an American landscape architect of the mid-nineteenth century who had written two books on house and garden design. Although he and Henry were contemporaries, Downing was the antithesis of Thoreau in architectural tastes, favoring elaborately decorated Victorian structures. Even before I read any of his books in depth I had come to appreciate Downing's designs, and I decided to build a house based on one of his gardener's cottages. It would be about the size of Henry Thoreau's cabin, ten feet by sixteen, but it would have board and batten siding, a steeply pitched Gothic roof, and a lot of gingerbread trim. The cottage quite suited my own philosophy of land use, which falls somewhere between the managed gardens of Andrew Jackson Downing and the wild, untamed nature of Henry Thoreau.

I drew up some rough plans; I bought the lumber from a local sawmill, one of the oldest continuously operating mills in the country. I purchased the nails, roofing, and other materials from the hardware store, and I began to search for used doors and windows. From a massive Georgian structure that was in the process of being refurbished, I managed to salvage some elegant narrow windows; I found heavy yellow pine French doors at a barn sale and some beautifully fashioned porch rails at a house that was being torn down. Finally, with all the materials more or less on the site, I began to build.

This dream of building a house of one's own is very nice in theory. But in fact, building is a maddening process. It requires a certain amount of skill in measuring. You have to handle cumbersome, dangerous tools. You are forever tripping over things, losing essential equipment, barking your knuckles, and lifting objects that are too heavy. I had had some experience in light construction. I once built a porch; I had made a greenhouse and a chicken house; but I would never in all the world claim to be skilled in carpentry. In fact I hate heavy work; I simply build things because it is often easier to do it oneself than to hire someone else. Fortunately, for this project, which was by far my most ambitious, I had help.

I had a friend named Higgins who lived on the banks of the Nashua River in Groton in a former stable, which he and his paramour, Jane, had retrofitted into a comfortable little yachtlike house. Higgins had a variety of talents. He had worked as a back-up musician, a yacht captain, a tow-boat operator, and, for a while, as a reader for a publishing company. He was also a carpenter. When I began thinking about building a house on my own, I called him for help, and with Higgins as a resource, I slowly came to understand the intricacies of the process.

One afternoon in early March he and I laid out the square for the foundation posts on the site I had selected in the hickory grove at the top of the ridge. That done, Higgins retired to other projects, and I spent one whole day digging the four holes, four feet deep, as he had directed. Higgins came back for a few hours one afternoon and helped me lay out the sills, and he returned on another day and showed me how to set up the frames for the ground floor, although I had to do most of the heavy work myself. The house was a sort of modified post and beam. I built frames for the ground-floor walls on the deck Higgins and I had constructed, and then, struggling mightily by myself, forced, pushed, hoisted, and otherwise raised the whole end of the house into place and temporarily nailed it with supports. It took me a day to raise the two gable ends, another to construct the two side walls, and a third to get them up and nailed in place. The whole boxlike affair was horribly unstable and rickety, but Higgins assured me that the frame would tighten up as the building progressed.

The project went slowly. I was working daily at my regular job, and I was taking care of my children while my erstwhile wife was in the process of launching herself in a new career. I was also, somewhat vainly, still attempting to enjoy the glorious spring that was by that time sweeping across the ridge. By mid-May, however, I was ready to put up the rafters. Higgins came back one weekend and taught me how to select the proper angle for the roof without using complicated mathematical formulas. We simply laid the actual rafters down on the deck; I chose an angle that I felt best suited the Gothic style of the house, and we cut them on the ground and nailed them together. That done, the two of us set about the precarious task of hoisting the rafters onto the ground-floor framework and setting them in place.

For all his skills Higgins is not good at math and measuring. Neither am I, and at one point we discovered (he discovered, to be more accurate) that we had miscalculated and somehow skewed the rafters by an inch or two. Since the whole frame would eventually be covered in ceiling material, and since the error would not affect the strength of the cottage, we carried on. All day and into the next, balancing ourselves on my swaying, unstable frame, we nailed rafters in place. When it was completed, at the end of that weekend, I could see for the first time what my cottage would actually look like. Higgins and I walked down the little driveway I had cut through the pine woods and looked back up the hill through the trees. There it was, a tiny chapel-like structure, standing alone among the hickories, the sassafras trees, and the white pines.

Higgins christened it "The Vicarage."

"I'll be back for vespers," he said.

I didn't expect him to return; he had done enough already, and he was one of those people who always take on more projects than they have time for. Once, twenty years earlier, I had worked on a boat with Higgins. He was first mate, and I was a lowly deckhand. He tried his best to snarl and act the part of a proper seafaring man, but I recognized in him a gentle soul, and we became fast friends in spite of our unequal rank. He knocked about in boats for years after that first summer, and then, horrified by the decline in interesting sailboats, put the proverbial oar on his shoulder and walked inland until someone asked him what that thing was. And there he settled, never again to go to sea.

Actually, he ended up in Groton because Jane lived there. They had known each other on Martha's Vineyard, which she had left some years earlier to go to film school. She was now a free-lance film editor, and, more to the point, she had been given an old stable not far from the Nashua River, a perfect place for Higgins to bide his time. One thing led to another; they fell in love (again) and set up housekeeping in the stable one summer while they fixed the place up. After three years the former stable had become a warren of hidden sleeping lofts, libraries, tiny pantries, and catwalks.

Higgins did come back again to help me with the roof. Together we planked the steeply pitched rafters and then, since time was running short for Higgins, we began shingling even before the side walls were built. Originally Higgins had tried to talk me into using cedar shingles, but I was running out of money by then as well as time. My self-imposed deadline of June 21 was closing in.

Still, things were moving along. Even though it had no walls, the house now kept out rain; it had the feel of a gazebo or a Japanese teahouse set at the edge of a mysterious wood. Over the next month I constructed the frames for the windows and doors, then planked up the sides and nailed battens along the seams in the popular Victorian style of Andrew Jackson Downing's designs. Working alone now, without the benefit of my mentor, I made slower progress but managed well enough. I could now actually see what had to be done, rather than conceptualize imaginary angles and shapes. I still had to measure, however, and I spent an inordinate amount of time cutting and recutting boards because of my incompetence at fractions.

One day in June I hung the French door. The house looked completed, and in fact I could have moved in, but there was a lot more to do. Using a borrowed saw, I cut filigreed bargeboards for the gable ends of the roof. I built tiny, Gothic-style trim boards for the many windows, and sawed out a decorative swan and nailed it above the front door. Once these important details were completed, once the floor was sanded and varnished and the windows screened and the front porch constructed, I was ready to take up residence.

I collected some of my favorite possessions: an antique parlor organ, a bed that had belonged to one of my brothers in his youth, a little desk I had grown up with, a few books, a mandolin, an antique French flute my mother gave me for my thirtieth birthday, paintings by my eldest brother, and old family photographs my father had taken during cruises on the Chesapeake Bay in the 1920s. My house in order, there could be no further delays, and right on schedule, on a sultry midsummer evening that smelled of soil and roses, I moved in.

2 In Two Worlds

THAT WAS A NOISY FIRST NIGHT, I remember. There was a terrific raccoon battle somewhere in the woods behind the house; the whippoorwills, which for years had arrived in the nearby woodlands in mid-June, called throughout the night, and I heard all manner of scratchings and scurryings around the house. At one point, just after midnight, a horrific scream sounded out, a ghostly yowl that started as a whine, increased in volume, and then crescendoed to a high pitch. Whatever it was went bounding off into the woods after its first scream, screeching and yipping as it went.

I sat up in bed under the window, listening. The scream had silenced the whippoorwills, and once the thing disappeared into one of the many hollows behind the house, the forest was silent again. The night was warm; a slight breeze rustled the tree tops, and I could hear whispers in the trees as if the leaves were talking to one another. I lay back and drifted off. From the distance came a single hoot, followed by a clatter which slowly grew louder, a train passing on the Portland-Ayer line that runs beyond the lake in back of the cottage. I listened as it approached, clacking and rattling, and then moved off to the north. Singly, then in twos and threes, the whippoorwills started up again, the breeze hissed in the leaves, a dog started barking on one of the farms over the hill — and I fell back asleep.

In spite of the interruptions of the night, I woke up refreshed. This was June 21, the first day of summer, and the sun was slanting in through the French door and spilling across the wide pine floor. Bird song was everywhere, rolling in through the open windows, and the cottage was filled with air and light and the fresh smell of the morning woods. Except for the fact that I had a roof over my head and screens on the windows, I might as well have had my bed out of doors, which of course was my intention.

I brewed some coffee and took it out to a sunny spot in the meadow to sit and think for a while. The raking light of early morning was spearing through the trees into the fresh green grass, and I could hear the long, bubbling call of the indigo bunting, one of the common bird residents on my patch of land. I drank coffee and landscape in alternating sips.

Henry Thoreau would have liked my domain, I thought. Houses, telephone wires, roads, and other intrusions of the modern world were nowhere to be seen. The wall of the forest surrounded the little meadow on three sides, and on the east the land was bordered by a low tangle of shrubs and young trees. A tiny footpath winding down through the meadow disappeared into the shrubs and continued on through the old gardens of my former house, where my children still lived. Here, on the back lot, I was isolated from the outside world, surrounded entirely by wildness, even though family and friends and civilization were close at hand. It was a quiet, private corner of the world, a good place to think. And yet it was an ironic landscape. This wild ridge, with its mysterious, forgotten forest, was located no more than thirty-five miles west of Boston, not far from Route 128, America's "Technology Highway," and a little more than a mile beyond Route 495, another beltway ringing the Boston suburbs.

I poured a third cup of coffee and sat back to listen to the chorus of birds. Towhees, thrushes, warblers, robins, and buntings were filling the woods with song. But as I listened, I became conscious of another sound. I could hear the dull roar of traffic on Route 495, as well as cars passing on another, smaller highway that ran southeast from the small towns of southern New Hampshire. As early as seven-thirty every weekday morning a great tidal surge of cars would sweep down that road. Car would follow car in a steady stream, each tailgating the others, their drivers rushing toward offices along the industrial belt that encircled Boston. Eight hours later, the tide would turn and the cars would flow back again to New Hampshire.

The volume of traffic on these local roads had increased significantly in recent years. The area where I had built my cottage was one of the fastest growing on the East Coast. New houses, new industries, were popping up everywhere, but my house was located in an empty quarter. Development had failed to cross the highway that separated the ridge from the rest of the town, so the woods, the old fields, and the farms of my immediate surroundings were still intact. But beyond this small, as yet undeveloped patch, the world was changing.

One of the largest new buildings occupied a hill on the other side of the valley east of my cottage. Long before I made plans to build my cottage, an obscure notice appeared in the local newspaper about a hearing concerning a new industrial building that was proposed for a site in a pear orchard just to the northeast of the town common. Digital Equipment Corporation, a multinational company that had grown enormously in the past few years, planned to construct in the orchard an industrial complex consisting of two immense office buildings, which would hold, upon completion, some four thousand workers.

Digital has a good reputation as an employer. It has promoted women and minorities, offers extensive employee benefits, rarely fires people, and offers flexible working hours. Furthermore, for a variety of reasons, some of which are economic rather than moral, the company does not accept military contracts. The fact that in the same year that I built my primitive dwelling, one mile away one of the fastest-blooming multinational corporations should construct a huge, sophisticated central engineering complex dramatically increased the irony of this already incongruous part of the world.

The site the company selected was one of the more scenic in the town. In the mid-nineteenth century, in the years when Henry Thoreau used to come occasionally to the town common, the owners expanded their farm. They sold off their dairy herd and planted an extensive orchard on a northwesterly slope just beyond the common. As late as the mid 1980s the orchard was still a thriving operation, and the flowering trees, the heavy fruiting of autumn and late summer, and the spidery landscape of the winter branches provided a pleasing contrast to the clutter of gas stations and shops that had sprung up around the town common in recent decades. But the orchard was a prime piece of real estate, and after holding on longer than many would have, with old age approaching, the owners were forced to sell.

There was a series of meetings about the proposed development in the town, none very well attended by the people of the community. No one seemed to care that a giant industrial building was about to be constructed just off the town common. The various town committees did their best to make sure that the development met all the state and local regulations and building codes. But, as there was no law prohibiting the construction of office buildings in pear orchards, the project moved along. A slight delay occurred when it was learned that the parking lot for the building was planned for an area that had questionable drainage, and for a while — for quite a while, in fact — company engineers and the local boards struggled to work out a compromise so that the parking lot could be constructed in such a way that the local water cycles could continue their ancient patterns. The Digital engineers, experienced in dealing with town boards, exhibited a certain resigned patience, and they dutifully designed and redesigned their plans to meet the local standards.

When I learned of the development, I became concerned about a number of barns and historic houses that were located on the property. One was an elegant eighteenth-century dwelling with two narrow stone walls bordering a long landscaped drive. There was also a great, sturdy nineteenth-century barn with a foundation constructed from immense granite boulders. And there was a tall, narrow outbuilding that I had coveted for years. My thought was to move it to my land if no one else wanted it.

The colonial house was saved as a conference center, but, driving through the town common one morning, I noticed a bulldozer parked in front of the barn — always an ominous sign. When I drove back through the common later that evening, a hole had appeared in the sky. The place where, for one hundred and sixty-two years, the barn had stood was level again; the great beams and posts had been carted off to some unknown fate, the huge granite foundation blocks presumably buried on the site. The tall outbuilding I had cherished had been smashed; I could see little bits of it piled here and there.

About a year before I began to build my own modest house, the construction crews broke ground for the Digital buildings. They sliced off the top of the hill; giant earth-dredging machines dug out an immense foundation; concrete trucks appeared, seemingly from all corners of the world, and slowly, week by week, throughout that year, in spite of the rains of autumn, the snows of winter, and the mud of spring, construction progressed steadily.

Later, when the steel frames were going up, I began work on my house, and for a while we worked in tandem. I raised a beam, and they, with their tall cranes and their sky hooks, set their I-beams. With rough-cut pine boards from the local mill, I sheathed my house in board-and-batten siding; they poured concrete and faced their structure with a thin layer of brick. I shingled, strip by strip, my steeply pitched roof. They poured some sticky waterproof substance over their vast flat-topped roof.

After I completed my cottage, I found — somewhat to my surprise — that I had fashioned exactly what I had drawn on paper: a high, neo-Gothic, chapel-like cottage. They had in turn constructed exactly what their designers had in mind, a square, low-slung building, which, in spite of its overbearing presence, somehow looked ashamed of itself. It was inordinately plain, neoindustrial, characterless, and so flat, so boxlike, so boring that I actually found it perversely interesting.

In spite of this intrusion, my cottage and the uninhabited ridge behind it proved an excellent refuge from the world at large. My house was decidedly primitive — I had no running water or electricity — but there was a satisfying, elemental comfort about life there. On certain evenings a deep, almost primeval silence would descend. Often in the midst of this vast stillness I could hear the high bark of foxes, the wailing of the whippoorwills, and the ghostly hooting of the barred owls that inhabited a swamp just to the south of the lake. With no street lamps or city lights nearby, the moon and stars seemed brighter, the sky blacker. Inside my house the light of the oil lamps cast a warm glow over the rough-cut pine walls, and in the peace of the long summer evenings I came to appreciate the beauty of shadowed corners, of silence and the uncivilized night. It was a curious existence. Here, in the very center of the expanding American electronics industry, I was living a sort of third-world existence, without modern conveniences, and surrounded by woods and old fields. It was a retreat into a closer wilderness, which was, to my mind at least, all the wilder for its very obscurity. I felt I was the only one who really knew the place.

Shortly after I moved into my cottage, I began keeping a record of the little events that occurred on my land. These notes soon evolved into something more than a simple account of the weather, or the blooming of flowers, or the arrival and departure of migratory birds. They became an exploration of the way in which I was living. Coincidentally, about the time I moved into my cottage I was given a full set of the 1906 edition of the journals of Henry Thoreau. Slowly, day by day, week by week,

I began reading through them and in time became consumed by the enigma of Thoreau's short life.

I had also collected that year a number of journals kept by various members of my family. My middle brother, Hugh, had sporadically written a journal; one of my cousins, who was something of an amateur naturalist, had kept meticulous, rather dry records of the natural history of his land on the Eastern Shore of Maryland; and my grandfather had periodically set down accounts of his daily life in the late nineteenth century. Most instructive, however, were journals kept by my father throughout most of his early adult years, including accounts of the years he spent in China between 1915 and 1918, and his life and travels in Europe and the United States in the 1920s and 1930s.

Together these various writings, along with my own modest records, covered a span of some one hundred and fifty years. Thoreau began his journal in 1837. My grandfather, who was over fifty when my father was born, began his in 1862. My father, who also started his family late in life, began his writings in 1911, when he was still in school; and my brother's and my cousin's journals covered the 1950s and 1960s. I came to realize that what I was reading was not so much daily notes on how people had lived in the world as accounts of the contracts that these individuals had made with the universe in order to survive. Skimming through them in anticipation of reading them more thoroughly over the winter, I realized that I was involved in a true Thoreauvian journey, an exploration of the private sea of being alone.

Within a week after moving into the cabin I had developed a pattern that would continue throughout the year. I'd get up as soon as the sun streamed in the east window, make coffee, carry it in a thermos to a sunny spot along the south wall, and sit there thinking and daydreaming. I came to love mornings at my cottage. Even though I had a regular job while I was living there, I seemed to have an inordinate amount of free time — partly,

I think, because I had no modern conveniences: no radio, television, or telephone to interrupt my thoughts. I enjoyed what some would consider the hardships of my existence — the lack of plumbing and electricity — and in fact I gained a healthy perspective on the way in which we live in our time. I would find myself marveling at common phenomena such as running water and instantaneous electric light. By contrast I came to relish the elemental experience of hauling water, trimming the wicks of oil lamps, and cooking over a camp stove or open fire.

Periodically the darker side of the miracle of modern technology would reassert itself, and I would become sharply aware that these are not the best of times. Quite apart from the fact that the superpowers continue to stockpile enough thermonuclear devices to obliterate the world, we seem to find ourselves in an age of environmental change that is matched only by the vast upheavals of prehistory — the extinction of the great land mammals at the end of the Pleistocene, the ice ages, the demise of the dinosaurs. In our time, toxic waste, the destruction of the world's tropical forests, global warming, the holes being eaten through the protective atmospheric layer, and other apocalyptic developments seem to be accumulating at an increasing rate. To add to the confusion, while I was living in my cottage I was immersed in the daily life of the nineteenth century through my reading. Henry Thoreau's journals gave me a sense of day-to-day life in Concord in the 1850s, and through my father's journals I was immersed in China at the beginning of the twentieth century. Almost every day that year I would pass through places in Concord that Henry had written about a hundred years before. And it seemed astonishing to me that my own father, the man I had known so well, had actually lived in Shanghai.

I am the youngest in my family by six years, the student, protégé, and victim of two energetic older brothers. My father, who was nearly fifty when I came along, was born in 1893 and grew up in a small town on Maryland's Eastern Shore. He went to Trinity College in Hartford, and then went off to China to teach English in Shanghai. He was a long-winded raconteur and a stickler for an orderly nineteenth-century way of life; our formal evening meals were often dominated by his singular, rambling accounts of China in the early part of the century or stories of his childhood on the Eastern Shore.

My mother, who was also from Maryland, was something of a renegade in her modest way. My father was an Episcopalian minister, but unlike many wives of ministers, my mother was not a joiner; she served on no committees and tried to stay clear of community affairs, preferring instead to put her energies into her teaching career. I began visiting her more often the year I lived in my cottage, and we would compare our memories of family dinners. The one thing we were able to establish was that my father, in the tradition of the old patriarch, tended to hold forth. I remember his rolling delivery, the deep voice, the carefully selected phrasing, the silences before the storms of his periodic outbursts of discipline, and his enduring view that there was something deep and serious behind the frivolity of daily life.

It was little wonder that he held this view in his adult years. Constantly he would come in contact with the tragedies of the town — deaths, alcoholic lives, troubled souls. But more to the point was his own past. During his first year in college, between Thanksgiving and Christmas, his parents died one after the other, and this shock, combined with the pressures of a freshman year in the alien North, threw him into a dark period of self-examination and struggle. It was after his graduation in 1914 that he left for China. He spent the next three years there. My mother used to say that he was trying to get as far away as possible from his past and his home. And indeed he came back from China sporting a nicely trimmed moustache, white ducks, and, according to his sister, speaking in an accent that was decidedly British — not an uncommon occurrence, apparently, for those returning from long stretches in Shanghai.

He seemed to have experienced a spiritual renewal in China. His own father had been a minister, so it was not surprising that he should choose the ministry himself. But before he went out to the Orient, before he was exposed to a world of civil war, poverty, and starvation, he was still casting about for a career. When he came back he went on to earn an advanced degree in English at Yale, and only then, after tutoring young people and knocking about in various university cities of the Northeast, did he decide to enter the seminary.

My father was able to endure an endless round of committee meetings and untold hours of personal counseling. Various lost souls in the community would regularly appear at our door and then disappear with him into his study to talk late into the night. He was deeply involved not only with his town and his flock but also with the larger world. He spent the summer of 1937 in Russia and western Europe. He stayed on Ukrainian collectives, and while he was in Germany heard the last sermon of Martin Niemöller, the famous antifascist Protestant minister: Niemöller delivered a fiery oration against Hitlerism, put away his notes, ended the service, and that afternoon was arrested by the Nazis.

My father returned from Europe a changed man. He became involved in politics and grew obsessed with history. During my childhood there was not a single evening meal at which some aspect of the past was not discussed in detail, either family history or world events. Night after night, in the large, high-ceilinged dining room, my father would spin out the pageant of time for us while, always in the background, I could hear the regular tick and chime of the antique French clock on the mantelpiece.

It seemed to me from all this that there was no escaping the overwhelming reality of change; the known world was coming to an end.

Yet, in the cottage, I was surrounded by bridges to the past. I had behind me in the woods the flourishing record of another age in the flowers of the dooryard gardens of farms long deserted. I would regularly pass through the Concord landscape of Henry Thoreau's journals; I had the handwritten accounts of people's daily lives; and I even had the artifacts of my father's past, the staff he had used when he climbed Mount Fuji in 1916 and a shard of a yellow tile he had picked up from the wall of the Forbidden City. I had my father's original editions of the books of the orientologist Lafcadio Hearn. Pressed in the middle of his copy of *In Ghostly Japan* I found a ginkgo leaf he had collected in a temple yard in Japan sometime in 1917. I had my father's photos of street life in Shanghai in 1916. I even had the camera he used to take the pictures.

One of the objects I remembered best was a peculiarly horrid piece of statuary that had taken on an almost magical power in my young mind. It was a small ebony figure of a squatting, baldheaded man, about six inches high. The man held in front of him a larger head, sliced off at the hairline and hollowed out to create a small bowl. The faces on both heads were Oriental, expressionless, serene, and ominous.

This object was moved from place to place in the house where I grew up. For a while it sat on a shelf in my father's darkened study, where north light spilled through the leaded glass window. It sat on his desk for a time. Then it was banished by my mother to an obscure shelf beside the stove in the kitchen, where it was used to hold matches, and finally it was moved to the attic and eventually disappeared.

The statue had the bitter smell of old ashes. The bowl held little bits of broken wooden matches, and if you ran your finger around the inside, it came out smudged and redolent of something evil. Once I dreamed about the head. Nothing happened in my dream except that the head seemed to have a power or life of its own. Years later, thinking about it, I came to realize that this hideous thing symbolized for me the entire experience of my father's years in the Orient. It was somehow the essence of time past, mysterious, dark, and profoundly attractive.

The summer I moved into the cottage I finally located the statue. One rainy July afternoon my eldest brother, Jim, who never intentionally throws anything away, brought it to me. It was inside an old cardboard box, wrapped in newspapers dated

1963, the year my father retired and moved from the rectory of his church. Layer by layer I unwrapped the papers, and there it was, nesting in the news of the past. The thing was smaller than I had remembered it; the dark wood seemed to have lost some of its sheen; and a crack I didn't remember had appeared on one side of the bowl. But it still seemed to carry with it all the memories of past lives.

3 Beside
the Green Meadow

BY EARLY JULY the forest and the fields surrounding the cottage were flourishing with a sustained vigor. Bird song was never so charged, the woods never so lush and sweet-smelling nor so alive with insect life. Butterflies drifted over the open areas; the meadow crickets began calling; the leaves were full, the grasses green and water-filled; and the buds of field wildflowers, which all through June had been swelling and filling, were in bloom.

Nowhere was this vigor of summer life more apparent than in the meadow beyond the stone terrace of my cottage. Just to the south of the house, rolling to the southeast in an easy slope, was a cleared area of an acre and a half, which, by early summer, had become a veritable jungle of grasses. I once counted some twenty different herbaceous plants growing there. On another occasion I discovered twelve dew-bejeweled webs of the orb web weaver spider glistening in the morning sun. I used to lie there on those spacious, early summer afternoons surrounded by the wall of woods and watch the wild sky play out its cloudscape overhead, and sometimes I would fall into a sort of reverie in which the restrictions of space would dissolve, and I would feel myself transported. Given a little leap of faith, I could imagine myself in some high pasture undisturbed by time and the twentieth century. There were periods when I would spend the entire day simply staring at things, rising occasionally to move my chair to some more favored spot in the meadow, following the sun and thinking vaguely that, sometime, I should get up and do something.

Five years before I moved to my cottage, the meadow was a pine forest, an entirely different and, in many ways, less appealing place — dark, rank with poison ivy, and essentially devoid of wildlife. In a survey that I made when the area was wooded with trees, I counted a patch of Canada mayflower, a few cucumber roots, and a great deal of poison ivy. Birds avoided the place, and only one mammal, a gray squirrel, nested there. Some forty years earlier the pine woods had been an orchard. In among the dark pines I could still see the decaying trunks of old apple trees. In its declining years, part of the orchard had been used as a dump by a family named Case who lived in the old house below the meadow, and before that the orchard had been a pasture for the family cow. Before the coming of the white man three centuries ago, the place had probably been forested with oak or white pine, the trees that make up the climax forest in this part of the world.

I have the more recent history of the area on the authority of a man named George Case, who appeared at the doorstep of my cottage that summer and explained that he had once lived on this land. Case's father had left home when George was about eight years old, and his mother moved her three children around from house to house until finally, in 1925, she restored her maiden name and moved back to her family home in Littleton. The Case house was small; downstairs there was a living room, a tiny birthing room where old man Case and his wife slept, and a kitchen wing. The upstairs was partitioned into several little cabinetlike rooms where various children of the extended family bedded down. By the late 1920s seven people were living in what was, in essence, a five-room house.

Old man Case, George's grandfather, was a sometime farmer who supplemented his income by working in a webbing mill in town. He kept a white horse in the apple orchard, had a pig, a flock of hens, and a noisy rooster named Fred. George and his cousins used to ride the white horse bareback around the apple orchard, but it was only half tame and would try to scrape the children off its back by galloping under low branches. The children became adept riders, wheeling off to the side and clinging to the horse's neck and body Indian fashion to avoid the trunks and limbs. On so small a farm there was not much work for the children to do, and whenever they couldn't catch the horse, they would wander the land around the house looking for excitement. George had a lot of stories about the forested ridge beyond the meadow, and, as we sat drinking coffee on the stone terrace in front of my cottage, he recounted them. Much of what he told me I had heard before, but I liked his slow, dreamy delivery.

One night, he told me, he and his cousins had slept out in the woods behind the orchard. They made a campfire and posted a guard to watch through the night, each taking turns.

"I'm sitting there on watch," he said, "and I hear this crunch, like a guy walking. I look up and I see this Indian with a spear standing there. Long leggings, bare chested. When he sees me look up at him, he bares his teeth and hisses, like a bat or something. I don't mind telling you I pissed my pants."

George screamed. His cousins woke up, searched the forest with flashlights and torches, but found nothing.

"But I'm telling you that I saw that Indian as clear as I see you now. Clearer, maybe. That was fifty years ago and I haven't forgotten yet."

The year he turned sixteen, shortly after the stock market crashed, George and one of his cousins knotted some sheets together, lowered themselves out an upstairs window, and hit the road. They ended up riding the rails to Oregon, found work as timber cutters, and after knocking about in various logging camps eventually settled down there. George married, continued to work for timber companies, and led an uneventful life, no doubt by choice; he had moved enough during his youth. This was his first trip back east since he had run away in 1930, and as we walked the land, he stared silently and shook his head in disbelief. "I remember good times here," he said at one point. What impressed him most was the pine forest just south of the meadow. The land had been a sunny field when he ran away; now it was penumbral and ominous.

A more natural man than myself — Henry Thoreau, for example — would have luxuriated in the return of the white pine forest. In Henry's time nearly 85 percent of New England was open fields, so it is little wonder that the forest fascinated him. In my time that statistic has reversed. Several years before I moved into the cottage I concluded that it would be a good thing to cut down the pine trees that had grown up on that part of my land and restore the pasture. My wife and I had met a woman who had a timber-cutting operation in which she used not heavy equipment — skidders, cherry pickers, and bulldozers — but mules, and when I decided to clear the pines, I called her up and struck a deal. She would leave me the hardwood for my woodpile and take the pine for herself to sell to a lumber company. It was a pretty even trade as far as I could calculate.

This mule-driving woman was not, as you might imagine, a raw-boned Amazon. She was about thirty years old, of medium build, with clear, soft skin and a mane of chestnut hair that she often wore in a single long braid. She was married to a timber operator who occasionally worked with her, but mostly she ran the business herself, marking the trees, cutting and trimming them, and then setting the tackle for her mules to drag the cut timber out of the forest to a loading area. She loved her mules with that kind of respectful love one might have for a large and powerful, perhaps slow-witted, child. She used to ride them, and in fact was a member of a hunt club in a nearby town, where she would appear among the properly attired huntsmen with their expensive horses and dogs on her favorite mule, Tulip, a great giant of a thing with ridiculous crooked ears. Once mounted she was one with her mule, a little like a female centaur.

One day, while I was dozing against a tree in a park, I saw her storm past, surrounded by a motley crew of hounds. She had let her hair out of its braid, and she thundered by me like a Valkyrie, the ground shaking under the hoofbeats of her mule.

For a while she worked as the dog warden for the town, and during that time was given charge of a full-blooded wolf that had been confiscated from someone in the state. She used to run the wolf on a long lead through the woods around Walden Pond and the town of Lincoln, and I would sometimes come across her, trotting along in her jogging shoes, with a huge yellow-eyed wolf at the end of a long tether. I got to know her wolf. It was the most terrified, timid thing I have ever met, shying away to the end of its lead whenever I stopped to talk.

Laura, the mule woman, arrived to clear my land with her mules and two male helpers. The men set to work immediately, felling trees, while Laura walked her team up the ridge to the area that was being cleared. She trimmed a couple of fallen pines, chained them together, and then hooked the chain to the mules and walked with them back to the road. Once she had repeated this procedure a few times, the mules had learned the routine. They would haul the logs down to the landing and wait there for Laura to come and unhook them.

What I had planned was essentially a clear cut, an anathema to some environmentalists. I intended to take out virtually every tree inside the three stone walls that surrounded the lot on the south, west, and north. The idea was to recreate the pasture of the late nineteenth century. But once the actual cutting started, I began to have some reservations about what we were doing to the forest. What right did I have to cut down innocent pine trees that had lived longer than I, and whose ancestors had been living in the area for some eight thousand years? Given the retreat of open land in New England in the present century and the return of the white pine forest, I had rationalized that cutting over a mere two acres of this overbearing, dismal woods to let in light and restore some of the nineteenth-century landscape would be a good thing. By clearing a small patch of land in the midst of a great sea of forest, I was creating an edge, a place for grass and herbaceous plants to grow, which would attract and provide food for birds, mammals, and insects.

Nevertheless, I watched with remorse as the mules hauled out the first of the tall fifty-year-old pines, brutally stripped of their feathery branches, quartered into movable pieces, and ignominiously stacked beside the road to be carried away and turned into — what? Boxes? Two-by-four studs that would be buried in the walls of some suburban tract house? My remorse deepened as the forest diminished, and when the two-acre lot became, in the space of a few days, nothing but an open, raw-looking wasteland with neat piles of brush stacked here and there, I had the sense of having done something horribly wrong and irrevocable.

Once the mill operator had hauled away the pine and the hardwood was cut, split, and stacked, I had to decide what to do with my clear cut. For a year I simply let the land heal, and I was surprised to see how quickly it recovered. A lot of poison ivy had been growing in the pine woods and along the stone walls, and as soon as there was a clearing, it began to spread furiously, along with blackberry, grass, cinquefoil, and goldenrod. By the end of that summer healthy young plants were growing everywhere. This was good for most of the local wildlife, and I felt somewhat vindicated for my rash act of tearing down the forest, even though the new growth made the place almost impassable for human beings.

Apart from the rank thicket of brambles and poison ivy, there were four unsightly piles of brush and stumps in the clearing — not exactly what I had had in mind for my meadow — so I gave up on all natural solutions and called in my archenemy, the bulldozer. In a single day a big yellow monster, in the hands of a grizzled man named Jim, dug out the stumps, buried them along with the slash, shifted a few boulders for me, and in the process ground down, uprooted, or otherwise destroyed the full two acres of blackberries and poison ivy. When he finally left, a peaceful silence descended over the clearing.

I let the area grow up again. First to return were the poison ivy shoots and the blackberries, which, although ground down to nothing on the surface, had their roots deeply set in the topsoil. But this time other species came along as well, and by the end of that growing season the lot showed more diversity of plant life than it had had in perhaps its entire previous history. Toward the end of that summer I counted the number of species in my first informal ecological survey. In subsequent years in the meadow I found brown snakes, red-bellied snakes, garter snakes, and milk snakes. I saw leopard frogs, pickerel frogs, wood frogs and toads, red-backed salamanders, katydids, meadow crickets, long-horned grasshoppers, and uncountable species of beetles. Foxes and skunks regularly crossed the meadow; deer grazed there; juncos, whitethroats, song sparrows, and tree sparrows garnered the weed seeds in autumn and winter. Robins and flickers were abundant; flycatchers darted from the trees along the edges to snap up the field insects flying above the ground; swallows coursed the clearing by day, followed by bats at night. There was light and air; stars, wind, and sky; life had returned.

I was not leading an entirely monastic life at my cottage in the woods. About a year before I moved in I had met a woman named Jill Brown who had recently separated from her husband, as I had from my wife. We used to go out to lunch together to commiserate. Then we began going out to dinner, and then we began going out in earnest. She smelled vaguely of cinnamon, and had a passion for French; she used to quote long, sad passages from Baudelaire. On weekends we would often go to concerts together, and during the week we would wander around looking for adventure. One evening in early July she and I were poking around the back streets of Concord looking at flower gardens and daydreaming of an orderly life, as compared to the disorderly one we seemed to be leading. We were passing along a picket fence when it suddenly struck me that we should visit Thoreau's grave. It was more than a thought; it was an imperative, something we had to do that very day.

In spite of the fact that I used to visit Walden Pond regularly, and in spite of my increasing interest in Henry and his way of life, I had yet to visit the spot on Authors' Ridge where he is buried, alongside Emerson, Alcott, and other luminaries of Concord.

We walked back through the center of town and out to the east, to Sleepy Hollow Cemetery. This was the most pleasant of summer evenings; an immense colony of swifts had nested in the chimneys of an insurance company near the town center, and as we passed, they were coming in to roost. They made a vast swirling funnel above the roof, circling like a storm and filling the air with their loud chattering as they prepared to enter the chimneys for the night. They were the only sign of life at that hour; the streets were curiously empty, the shops closed and sad. We walked up through the darkening grounds of the cemetery and then climbed the steep, short hill to the ridge and the grave sites.

Quite fittingly, Henry was buried without pomp among the members of his family. Central in the grouping of gravestones is the marker for his mother and father, who are surrounded by their four children, all of whom died without issue. Even though the stone itself was indistinguishable from the others, Henry's grave stood out. Pilgrims had been there before us that day and had laid bunches of flowers at his tombstone, while the other small markers were barren. We stood there for a while, thinking about the family.

The sun had long since set, but a warm, smoky light held in the sky above the trees. Under the branches, on the hill, and among the surrounding monuments there was a cathedral-like gloom. I read the simple inscription on Henry's gravestone: "Henry D. Thoreau July 12, 1817–May 6, 1862."

"What is the date today?" I asked Jill.

"July twelfth," she said.

I began to suspect that this Henry Thoreau was becoming more entwined with my life than I wanted.

On July 4, 1845, the year he turned twenty-eight, Henry moved into his house at Walden Pond. He borrowed a wagon from a friend, loaded it with his few earthly belongings, and hauled everything out through the woods to the door of his newly constructed dwelling. He did not own much. As he tells us in *Walden,* he had at the cabin a table, a bed, three chairs, a three-inch looking glass, and a tent, which he kept rolled in the loft. He also had three plates, a cup, a spoon, two knives and forks, a japanned lamp, a flute, a kettle, a skillet, a dipper, and a washbowl. He brought with him a few cherished books, including his copy of *The Iliad,* and some lighter reading.

The cabin was not actually completed when he moved in. The walls had yet to be plastered, and there were wide chinks between the secondhand boards he had used for siding. He claimed to enjoy the flow of air through these chinks, although he does not tell us what he did about the infernal New England mosquito.

July in New England lends itself to outdoor living. Henry had yet to build his fireplace, and he did virtually all his cooking over a campfire outside his front door. When it rained, he constructed a shelter over the fire and went right on baking. He loved bread, and he tried various experiments with different grains until he found the proper combination. He ate sparsely, swam regularly, roamed the nearby forest, chased foxes, and lived, as he says, close to the bone. It was an intense, focused life, stripped of luxury.

He got his water for drinking and washing from Walden Pond. He would also bathe there, sometimes twice a day, once just after he woke up and once after he had finished working in his nearby bean field. Presumably he washed his few dishes there as well. Somewhere near his cabin he had a privy, although as one of his biographers, Walter Harding, points out, he was too prudish, even in his wild, elemental state of mind, to tell us anything about it.

After his morning bath Henry would meditate on his natural surroundings and then tend the bean field he had planted, or continue in his meditations. In the field he would work barefoot until the day grew hot and the sandy soil burned his feet. Then he would wander off into the forest looking for plants and animals, and sometimes spend the rest of the day there, observing the diversity of the natural world. Later in his life, after he left Walden, he would become more methodical about these observations, more scientific, but at this point he seemed simply in awe of things. Every day he wrote in the journal he had begun in 1837, and it is the record of these days — the thoughts, the observations, and the accounts of his small adventures — that became the core of *Walden*.

Often in the afternoon he would walk to Concord, there to catch up on the news, which, from the comfortable distance of his Walden retreat, he was able to view with some remove. Any more involvement in daily life might have oppressed him. He would talk to townspeople, visit his family and friends, and often stay for dinner, either with his mother and sisters or with the Emersons.

After dinner he would walk home to Walden through the darkened woods. He grew to love these lonely, homeward-bound passages, the mist and dankness of the night woods, the darkness of the forest. He would feel his way between the trees, sensing, rather than seeing, the soft path.

His was an idyllic existence, the model balance between sociability and privacy, with space enough to think and feel and write. The idea of Thoreau as a loner, an eccentric, is more the result of nineteenth-century rumors about him than actual fact.

Although he was criticized by uncomprehending townspeople, he was not friendless, he was not alone, and he was not a drunk, as was commonly believed among the less-educated people of Concord. Furthermore, he was happy. He lived between two worlds, a city of muskrats to the south and, to his north, the town of Concord. He would visit both to observe the inhabitants, and, although he was critical of men and not of muskrats, he clearly enjoyed the spectacle of the town. He was no mountain man, this Henry Thoreau. He was a literate American, a social critic, and he needed a village.

Henry seems to have lacked direction in his early life. All things fascinated him equally. He was an inveterate researcher; he filled his journals with notes on trees, fruits, fish, geology, measurements, Indians, travels, people, and almost anything else he came across, but it was not clear to what end he was working.

Henry never fit in very well with his schoolmates in Concord, and he was something of an outsider at Harvard. When he graduated in 1837, jobs were hard to come by in Concord, but he was lucky and managed to land a teaching position at the local school. He lasted two weeks.

Henry and his brother, John, who was also a teacher, had ideas about education that were unusual for their time. Henry brought some of these views with him to the public school system. He was opposed to corporal punishment, for example, and did not, as was the custom in those times, thrash his pupils. The school officials, hearing about this odd behavior, made a visit and directed him to beat the students. So Henry lined them up, arbitrarily selected a few, and thrashed them. Then he quit.

A year later, in 1838, he and his brother started a school in Concord, one that shunned corporal punishment and followed an experimental curriculum that involved outdoor excursions. But after three years, partly because John fell ill, they closed the school, and Henry left teaching forever.

Always adept in the practical arts, after his school failed he helped his family improve its pencil-making business, and by the

1840s he had totally refurbished the operation so that it was one of the most profitable and prominent pencil factories in the East. But Henry had no abiding interest in manufacturing or business. What he really wanted to do was write.

He had written essays in college, and for years had fancied himself something of a poet, but he had had little published and had made virtually no money. In the spring of 1843, at the urging of his friend and mentor Ralph Waldo Emerson, he went to New York City to try to establish himself. But that, too, failed, and in the fall he was back home in Concord, never again to leave for any length of time.

He worked in his family's pencil factory the following year. He also wrote in his journals, took his walks, and occasionally went on excursions with his friends. On one of them, a boating trip up the Sudbury River, he and a companion accidentally started a forest fire that burned over the precious wood lots of several local farmers. By this time Henry had a reputation in Concord: a Harvard man who had never held a regular job, a writer who did not earn money for his efforts, a malingerer, an eccentric, a nature lover, and now a fire starter. And then, as if to confirm all the rumors, in the spring of 1845 Henry commenced the most rash act of his life.

For several years he had felt that what he needed to become a writer was time and space. He had thought about building a small cabin on the shores of Flint's Pond (now Sandy Pond) in Lincoln, but old man Flint, the owner of the pond, had refused to allow him to live there. In the hope of encouraging Henry in his writing career, Emerson offered to let him use some land he owned by the side of Walden Pond. Henry's move to Walden on July 4, 1845, marked the beginning of his career. It also marked the foundation of a philosophy.

Thoreau was not the first to live apart in order to delve into the heart of things, but he became the prototype for those who followed him. One does not live alone in a cabin in the woods and escape comparison with this man; and the longer I lived in my little Gothic cottage, the more I tried to counter his pure, spartan existence, the more I noticed that I too was under his influence. The trouble with Henry Thoreau is that, in so many ways, he got there first.

I found myself following a pattern that recalled Henry's. I would rise early in the morning and watch the unfolding of the dawn. These were for me, as they were for him, the finest hours of the day. Morning ablutions for me, however, were not quite so simple as they were for Mr. Thoreau. I was not so fortunate as to have a pond at my front door, although from time to time on hot mornings I would run down through the woods below my house and jump into Beaver Brook, which slides east below the ridge on which my house was perched. Washing myself and my dishes was slightly more complicated than it was, probably, for Henry. I rigged a primitive plumbing system in the cottage by installing a large water container in the loft and then running a pipe down to the kitchen corner, where I kept a small camp stove and a large copper urn to hold water. I would haul the water to the house in five-gallon jerry cans and horse them up the ladder to the loft to fill the tank. This primitive system of running water became something of an attraction. Visiting children, who in their daily lives would rarely drink anything as boring as water, would regularly draw off a cup from my copper urn. There is something fascinating about simplicity. Children know that. So did Henry.

Showers were another matter, as were regular meals. I commonly cadged both at Jill's house, from other friends, or at my old house. That year, once my erstwhile wife took up her new career, my child-care responsibilities increased dramatically. During the week I would often cook dinner for my children and myself at my wife's house. Weekends I got in the habit of eating breakfast at my cottage, followed by a walk in the nearby woods and fields. I would also hold alfresco dinners for friends in my meadow, and on some evenings we would sit there late into the night, talking, slapping at mosquitoes, and watching the fireflies and the stars.

I got a lot of advice from well-meaning friends after I moved into my cottage. Some suggested I run a wire up from my old house and install electricity. My brother Jim thought it would be a simple matter to run a garden hose up the hill to supply myself with running water. One person suggested, before I built, that I should simply get a trailer and park it in the woods. One of my constant advisers in matters of survival was a man named Mason who lived in the nearby town of Carlisle. He had fitted his house with a number of ingenious alternative devices for supplying himself with running water and electricity without reliance on the local light and water companies. Mason was an intermediary between the third world and the industrialized world. Lanky, with silky reddish-blond hair, habitually dressed in cotton or wool, he had a viewpoint on everything, including how to live in my house.

We took a walk together one day out to the hemlock grove behind the house. On the way back we passed a small, temporary wetland not far from my cottage. He halted and dug a hole with a stick.

"You know, you could drill a good shallow well by hand right here," he said. "You could have running water. For that matter you could have hot water. You run the water into the house, fork the pipes, run one section through copper tubing wrapped around your stovepipe, set it up with a tank, and you'll have hot water all winter."

"What will draw the water up from the well?" I asked.

"Electricity."

"But I don't have electricity."

"Get a bank of car batteries," he said. "Once a week or so you carry one out and get it charged while the others do the work. You could get car radios for your house, speakers, lights. You could even get a TV."

"I don't want a TV," I said.

"Well, that's great," he said. "That's cool. I don't want one either. But if I did . . ."

Briefly, very briefly, I had considered the idea of trying to live a true back-to-the-land, self-sufficient way of life. The land certainly would have been able to sustain me. I had at least two arable acres, a small woodlot that could have provided a continuous supply of firewood, and, perhaps most important, I had the model of the past. For who knows how many generations, people who had lived in the immediate area not only had fed themselves by farming but also had grown enough to make a decent living. There were a couple of obstacles to my doing so, however, the main one being personality. I once read a profile of the successful self-sufficient farmer, and he or she (usually both, working as a team) turned out to be the opposite of me. The ones who succeeded, according to the survey, were introverted, somewhat antisocial, more comfortable with machines than with people, happy to work long, lonely hours all day. I loved working the land, growing flowers and vegetables, lonely dawns, hand tools and hard work, and a few introspective hours every day. But I also had come to cherish the diversity of the human community in urban areas, which is why I ended up outside Boston instead of in Alaska.

Once, during the early 1970s, because of energy shortages, I attempted to live in a largely self-sufficient way. I had a large garden filled with staples such as corn, peas, and potatoes; I had a fine fat pig, a flock of good hens, asparagus beds, row upon row of herbs of all varieties, plus the usual staples such as cucumbers, squash, and tomatoes. I even grew rye and buckwheat one year and ground my own flour. It was a tidy little system, but it was hard work, and after a couple of years I noticed that a curious change had come over me. Before this experiment I used to revel in all kinds of weather. I would go out in sleet and snow; I loved to walk in rain; I enjoyed bad weather and would swelter with pleasure in prolonged, cricket-loud droughts. But once I started growing things seriously, I began to worry about the weather. I would feel uncomfortable in drought; I came to hate bean-soaking, fungus-nourishing rainy seasons; I watched the sky fanatically. In short, I stopped enjoying nature. By the time I built my cottage I had learned my lesson. I planted and weeded my flowers and vegetables and let the season decide which would live and which would die.

During those years when I had conducted my experiment in self-sufficiency, I became interested in appropriate technology. I had met a man named Charles MacArthur, who had concerned himself with energy conservation issues since the early 1960s — long before they became fashionable. He was forever organizing events to advertise the efficiency of alternative energy systems. One such event was a car race in which the winner was not the first to cross the line but the one who covered a given distance with the least expenditure of energy.

Among Charles MacArthur's many abiding interests were toilets. He was one of the first in this country to install the Swedish Clivus Multrum composting toilet in his house, and he had had a number of run-ins with boards of health because the toilets were not technically legal, according to local bylaws. Some years ago MacArthur moved his small-scale technology operation from Connecticut to Dover-Foxcroft, Maine. He bought a defunct mill, put it back into operation, and began supplying electricity to himself, as well as to the town.

Long before he moved to Maine, as a part of his research on composting toilets, he and an associate at the Smithsonian Institution ran across a set of nineteenth-century patents for an English device known as Moule's earth closet. This ingenious toilet was simplicity itself. It was a box about four feet by four feet with a seat on top and a door in the back which opened onto a bin located below the seat. The system ran not on water but on peat moss. After using the toilet, one simply emptied a few cupfuls of peat into the box. Periodically the peat had to be extracted and composted for eight weeks or so. After that the compost could be reused in the bin, or used to fertilize a garden. MacArthur found that these toilets had been in use for a time in this country, and that they had worked. So he built one.

I saw his earth closet once in Dover-Foxcroft, in a museum of modern and nineteenth-century energy-efficient and water-conserving designs that he kept in his mill; it was one of his prize displays. Somewhat to my horror, he opened the bin of the toilet he had designed (and used), picked up the compost in his hands, crumbled it, and invited me to smell it. It had a rich, earthy smell, a little like the soil in a freshly turned garden.

Although he knew the earth closet had been sold in the United States, MacArthur was unable to find an original. He searched antique stores and museums, and while he found thousands upon thousands of chamber pots in all manner of fanciful designs, he could not locate an earth closet.

There were a number of outbuildings connected to MacArthur's mills, and one day he decided to clear out one of the buildings to make room for a new project. Amid the clutter of nineteenth-century paraphernalia he found a hinged box that had once carried a high varnish. The thing looked suspiciously familiar to him, so he cleaned it up. Beneath the layers of caked soot and grime, he found the brand name written in that elegant false hand-lettering of nineteenth-century advertisements: "Moule's Earth Closet."

Toilets have never overly fascinated me, but this story of MacArthur's earth closet stuck in my mind, and shortly after I moved into my cottage, I constructed one of my own. At one end of an earth-floored lean-to in back of the house, I dug a shallow pit in the soft piney soil. I built a box with a side door over this pit and lined it with peat moss and lime to make my very own outdoor version of Moule's earth closet. I never told the board of health about this. The earth closet was probably as illegal as Charles MacArthur's Clivus Multrum had been back in Connecticut. But it worked better than many of the septic systems in the town, which, whenever it rained, spewed a noisome effluvium onto lawns and streets. I had to clean out my earth closet only twice that year. I turned the compost into the garden, and in the rich humus I grew a rank garden of cosmos, stock, cleome, snapdragons, and perennials.

I used to spend a lot of time in the mornings and then again in the evenings working in the garden. Living outdoors as I was, I gained a new appreciation of the subtle beauties of the change from day to night; the lonely, sparkling song of the wood thrushes and the veeries; the soft light, the fading colors. Often, after it was too dark to work in the garden, I would sit on my front porch and watch the display of the rising fireflies above the meadow. They made bright sparks against the black background of the night forest, brighter, it seemed to me, than anywhere else in the world, except, perhaps, the Eastern Shore of Maryland, where I first watched them.

My father liked fireflies. We used to spend summers on the Eastern Shore at a rambling nineteenth-century summer house known as the Reed's Creek place. It was set in the middle of a small grove of cedars and was surrounded by hay fields that rolled down to a wide creek where we kept a number of boats and a swimming dock. Often in the evening my father would go out onto the verandah on the west side of the house and sit in a rocking chair to watch the fireflies rise over the hay fields. He would reminisce about the Orient at these times and would often tell us the Japanese fairy tale of Princess Firefly. According to the legend, she was the most beautiful princess in the kingdom of the insects and had many suitors, none of whom she fancied. In order to hold them at bay, she announced that she would marry the one who was able to bring her a light that could match her own brilliance, and so all the lowly suitors rushed off to burning lights to try to steal fire. To this day they can be seen, still battering themselves against the light, still hopeful, after all these centuries.

No doubt my father picked up this story from the writings of Lafcadio Hearn, who was one of the foremost interpreters of

Japanese culture and the first person to collect the disparate folk tales and legends of Japan. While he was in the Orient, and perhaps even before, my father began reading Lafcadio, and years later, when he returned from the East and went on to graduate studies in English, he wrote his thesis on Lafcadio Hearn's fascination with the supernatural. It was an odd choice. Lafcadio was a gifted linguist, a skilled translator, intensely interested in exotic cultures, in the mystic, the sensuous, in folklore, nature, and the dark side of human experience. My father, although fluent in Chinese, was not particularly interested in language, folklore, mysticism, or nature. His Protestant religion was decidedly earthly; he was far more involved with people than transcendent spiritual experiences. And yet there was something of the exotic Lafcadio within him, some of which he managed to pass on to me. Part of this I may have absorbed from the collection of Hearn's works that I tried to read while growing up. Some of it may have sunk in during those lingering evenings on the night porches of the Eastern Shore while the starlike bursts of the fireflies flashed over the summer hay fields.

Even there, however, on those peaceful evenings, my father's voice would occasionally deepen into other tones, and we would know that we were about to be reminded of some tragedy — the plight of the Jews, the poverty of the Chinese, or the devastating power of the nuclear weapons that even then, in the innocence of the 1950s, seemed to him to be threatening the world.

4 Scyther's Complaint

 SOMETIMES IN THE EARLY MORNING, while the dew was still on the grass and the air was still cool, I would mow the grasses in the meadow. I kept an old scythe hanging on the back of my cottage, and regularly that summer I used it to keep the grasses down. I never scythed with the singleness of purpose of the old-time mowers, who would rise on a given day, and, working in a crew of men and boys, cut an entire hay field before breakfast. I preferred to mow at leisure, working up from the lower end of the meadow to the western wall. In this manner, cutting a little each day, I never really finished — one section would grow back before I reached the end of the field — but at least I had time to daydream while I worked.

Scything is for me one of the consistent small pleasures of life; the quiet swish of the blade, the fresh scent of new-cut grass, the little flights of retreating insects, and the sight of dew-dappled stems have a calming effect on me. Scything through a grassland in early morning, surrounded by bird song and the chatter of insects, offers a continuity with the past that few other occupations provide.

The scythe was developed with the cultivation of grains some five or six thousand years ago and evolved into its present form sometime in the twelfth century. It has voyaged through history with us, and only now, in recent decades, has fallen into disfavor, yet another victim of mechanization. But for my purposes, it is an eminently practical tool.

In virtually all the houses I have lived in, most of them in rural or semirural areas, the lawn was a rough expanse that had been neglected by the previous owners and had evolved into a meadow of wildflowers. Over the years I came to love these wild lawns. They were far more interesting to me than a clipped greensward, devoid of all but a few species of grass and perhaps an ant or two. Maintaining these meadows to keep them from returning to brush was a problem, however. Once or twice I tried to cut the high grasses with a power mower, but it was noisy, hot work, and when I was done, where there had been a tangle of life, nothing remained but a brownish swath of severed grass stems. I quit using mowers years ago and began cutting with a scythe.

One morning I was scything a small clearing down by the road below my cottage when my old friend Sven walked by.

"Cutting in the old way are you?" he asked in his lilting Swedish accent.

Sven was in his mid-eighties, and was an inveterate walker. I would often see him out on the road that runs along the eastern edge of the ridge, and I used to talk to him about the old days in Sweden. Ever since I first learned the art of mowing I have been interested in different scything styles, and I asked Sven to show me how he used to cut hay back home. He picked up the scythe and began cutting — not in a straight line, as we do in this country, but in an ever-widening circle.

There was another scyther in the neighborhood who had a curious style — my friend Megan Lewis, the woman who had the reputation of causing plants to flourish just by staring at them. She lived in an old house on the western slope of the ridge, and she also mowed her grounds with a scythe.

Early on a Saturday morning not long after I had talked to Sven, I went over to her place for a visit. On the southwest side of the ridge about twenty years ago timber operators had cut over a section of the slope, and the area had grown up into an impassable thicket. Megan lived on a direct line on the other side of the tangle, but to get there I always had to skirt the thicket, cut through one of the little hollows, and then take the old carriage road through a hall of dark pines to her property. She owned about forty acres, including two hay fields which she rented out to local farmers. I would come upon these first, beautiful little clearings surrounded on four sides by woodlands. Beyond, on the west side, there was a thin woods of larger trees, and beyond that were Megan's gardens, all of them in varying degrees of cultivation — tangled berry patches, a small nursery and seed bed for shrubs and young trees, a lonely little fountain overgrown with English ivy. Here and there stood a mossy garden statue. Beds of untended flowers were interspersed with newer plots and patches of mowed ground. In one of these plots I found Megan herself, leaning on a rake. She was in some ways a human version of her gardens — half-tended, her hands dirty with good soil, strands of gray hair falling from under a straw hat, and bits of grass and seeds clinging to her. She was dressed in her customary shirtwaist dress, which she seemed to wear whenever she was out working in her garden, as if the sacred act of gardening required proper attire. Sometimes, in fact, she seemed dressed for church whenever she gardened, but she was a considered pantheist, having long before rejected formal religion.

I told her I had seen Sven and he had shown me how in Sweden they had cut fields in a circle.

"Is he that old man you see walking to town with his shirt off sometimes?" she said.

"The very one."

"Now there's a good man. What does he do?"

"Well, he grows potatoes and zucchini, eats dinner at midday, and walks to town once a day. That's about all I know, except that he grew up on a farm in Sweden and worked as a groundskeeper for someone after he came to this country."

"Well, he's a good man," she said again. "The world needs more walkers."

She went back to raking, letting me know, without saying so directly, that she had no time to talk to me that day. I said goodbye and moved on.

"Come again," she said.

"You come to my house," I said. "You must see my little gardener's cottage I've built behind my old house. You'll like it. I stole the design from Andrew Jackson Downing."

"Well, it must be good then. I'll come."

There were a lot of rumors about Megan Lewis in the community. The most prevalent was that she had been an actress in New York City in the late forties. She had had a modest success on the stage, it was said, but quit because of some scandal and retired to the country. People also said that in the 1950s there had been a constant flow of exotic guests from the big cities at her place. One morning one of the farmers who lived nearby saw a man in robes standing in his pasture declaiming Shakespeare to one of his cows. This same farmer claimed to have seen a horse-drawn carriage filled with "actors and actresses" in period costumes on the deserted road that ran between the highway and the lake on the west side of the ridge.

I remember well my first conversation with Megan. "We heard you have been cutting your lawn with a scythe," she said to me. "We heartily approve. I am sick to death of these noisy, smoking motors. They scare the rabbits and the mice."

Megan always used "we" — the royal "we" — referring, I supposed, to her husband, Charley, a man rumored to be a lawyer, but who seemed to spend most of his time repairing their house, with little to show for his efforts. The place was a wreck, the talk of the town. It was a marvelous conglomeration of architectural styles, starting with the colonial period and ending sometime in the 1930s. It was an accumulation of wings and porches and connecting sheds and barns, not one of which was entirely painted or perfected, but each of which was in the process, ap-

parently, of being fixed up. "I like puttering" is the way Charley
once explained his various projects to me. "To be finished is
death."

Although Megan complained about their house, her gardens
were in a similar state. She was forever digging up one bed of
flowers to replace it with another of some other kind, and she
seemed to have a horror of the close-cropped, neatly tended
suburban yards that were fast becoming common in the town.
"Charley's failures notwithstanding," she said, "I do indeed prefer these old ruinous barns to the new face in this town. Laurels
and yews, yews and laurels — and clean green lawns. My God,
can they think of nothing else to plant?"

She was outspoken and opinionated, a woman of sensible shoes
who knew all the songs of local birds and frogs and who used
to allow the blacksnakes and milk snakes to winter in her cellar.
"They hate the cold as much as I do, poor things," she said.

Normally Megan and I would talk in her yard. But one November afternoon she invited me in for tea. Charley and Megan
had an English cast to their personalities. Tea was one of their
many small rituals, and it was done properly in fine old pots,
with bone china cups and saucers, and a little "bicky," as Charley
called his tea biscuit.

It was at one of these teas that I learned that, appearances to
the contrary, Charley and Megan had led a rather normal life,
up to a point. They had two grown children; and Charley had
indeed been a lawyer in Boston for some thirty years before he
retired. On weekdays he would commute into the city from their
"place," and on nights and on weekends and holidays he would
revert to putterer. I suspect he was not comfortable in either
world.

Megan was from New York, although she had lived in England
for years in her youth and also in Tunisia. She had learned
gardening from her mother, but early on she had thrown out
traditional designs and attempted to bring to her land what she

called her "wildings" — wildflowers that grew in the woods and old fields around her property.

"I gave that up soon enough," she told me. "It was a big mistake, I can tell you. These things have their place in the world. You tear them out, and they may or may not survive. But that's not the point. We have to learn to let things alone."

She replanted, for the second time in her life, a traditional English country garden, with hollyhocks and delphiniums and foxgloves all along the little winding paths, which she kept mowed with a scythe. After that she let these newer plantings grow old, and then she more or less had what she wanted.

"Eschew order. That's what I say. Controlled disorder is the most harmonious landscape. Just look about you. Just look at the woods."

Megan had had a hard year. Charley had died of a heart attack not long before I started building my cottage, and she had been spending a lot of time with her daughter, who lived near the Adirondacks. I hadn't seen much of her during the time I lived away from the ridge, but since their house was rarely empty — students, renters, family members, and weekend guests who somehow stayed on for months were always living there — I presumed she must have had plenty of company and solace. But she did come to my cottage after I invited her.

One Sunday morning in August, when Jill Brown and I were eating breakfast in the meadow, I saw Charley's old Peugeot tentatively poking its nose up the rutted driveway. Megan got out of the car slowly, fixed her hat, and began walking toward the cottage, not looking at anything, as if she had been there a thousand times. We hailed her from the meadow and she wandered over, but she was as distant as she had been the morning I invited her to come by. Jill had known Megan for years — in fact she had introduced me to her — but still Megan seemed oddly formal. There were none of her usual opinionated asides, no nasty little comments about the slow destruction of the town

or about incompetent or corrupt local officials. She inspected
the modest beginnings of my garden along the stone wall on the
west side of the property and politely withheld comment. She
had toast and coffee with us. She made small talk, but she seemed
profoundly bored. Yet she didn't leave.

I began to tell her about some problem I had had while building my house, and was in the middle of a sentence when she
broke in and changed the subject. "But this is actually quite nice
back here," she said, as if surprised. "You've got a crazy, mad
way of life, simply building a little house back here behind your
family when you have to separate — if you must separate. I
mean, this is very good I suppose. Good for the children." I saw
Jill look up at her.

"They love it here," I said.

"Well they might," Megan said. "And this woods. You don't
let them go out there alone do you? All those nasty teddy bears
and their picnics. You should stay on here," she said. "I mean,
I don't know whether you mean to have a temporary place for
yourself, but I wouldn't leave here if I were you. You've got to
hang on to things."

She picked up her empty coffee cup and put it down again.
I poured her more from the pot by the fire.

"Well, I really must go now," she said.

"Come again," Jill said. "We always have Sunday morning
breakfast here, except when it rains."

"But it is lovely here," Megan said. "I want to tell you something." She sat down, gathered her cup against her chest, but
said nothing.

"I've become addicted to this place," I said.

"It's a good addiction."

"Sometimes I dream about the woods."

"I do, too. I dream that Charley is in there in the woods and
I go looking for him and we meet. But I always have to leave,
and he has to stay in there." She paused. "Oh, my, I am sorry
to bore you."

"Not at all," Jill said. "We understand."

"But it is lovely. And you die, you know, when someone dies. I just want to say that. It's flat — the sky, the garden, the world itself — just flat. But for some ungodly reason your heart keeps on beating and you eat and you sleep badly and you wake up and eat again and all the while the world just goes on."

"Well, now, I am really going," she said. "But it doesn't need you, you should know that. This world I mean." She nodded toward the dark wall of the woods behind us.

I saw Jill's hand dart out to Megan's arm; Megan was on the verge of tears.

"I love this ridge," I said awkwardly. "I love this black wall of forest at midday. This is really one of the plainer pieces of land around here, probably. But you live here, you get to know it, and it has draw."

"It has its draw indeed," Megan said, quietly.

"Sometimes I have a feeling that this place, this actual spot where we are sitting is the center of the universe. It seems to me that anything can happen here — the beginning and the end . . ."

She broke in again: "You are right; it is the center. But it doesn't need you. I'll tell you that much, it goes on in spite of you. And that's its power."

"What power?" Jill asked.

"To restore."

She was quiet again, and then she said dreamily, "Restore thy body and soul." She laughed.

"I haven't been to church in fifty-five years, save when we buried Charlie. But I guess I have a religion. Quiet moments in a garden. Time in the garden. I suppose you would call it sacredness."

I had dinner one evening that same month with Higgins and Jane. After dinner we talked about the various ways in which different people, including homeless families, manage to survive.

In passing Jane mentioned an old man who lived without electricity or running water in the house in which both he and his father had been born. It turned out she was talking about a man I already knew, Sanferd Benson of Concord. Jane was worried that Sanferd was going to die soon and take with him all his knowledge of nineteenth-century ways. She wanted to make a video tape of his story. Sanferd was profoundly shy, suspicious of even such simple technologies as a still camera (I took a photograph of him once and I could tell he was uncomfortable). In any case I agreed to talk to him about the project since I used to visit him regularly.

I walked down the dirt road to Sanferd's place a few days later, but as usual he wasn't at the house. In an upstairs window a ragged shred of curtain was blowing in the wind, little swirls of dust were rising and settling in the sandy driveway, and a screen door was swinging loose. The only cars were the dead wrecks in the surrounding fields, parked there by Sanferd's car-loving nephew. Sanferd was never around when I went looking for him; he would simply materialize, as if he had been watching all along from some hiding place.

I found him in his strawberry patch, down the road from his house toward the Concord River. Sanferd was half blind; he wore smoky glasses he had repaired with tape and glue and little bits of wire, and he was tragically frail. He dressed always in baggy coveralls and a grim, blue-gray work shirt that smelled, even in summer, of kerosene and wood smoke, and he was rarely clean-shaven.

Sanferd was a man of limited horizons. He was born the same year as my father, 1893, and although he lived only a few miles from Concord Center, he was one of the most sheltered, isolated people I have ever met. He had lived on the same small farm all his life, hardly ever left Concord, had never married, and, from what he told me, rarely even left home. Once a week in the early part of the century his father would take the wagon into town to buy supplies and Sanferd would go with him, waiting patiently at the store counter to be offered some small favor by his father or the shopkeeper. His primary connection with the outside world was the Concord River, which flowed past his land about two hundred yards from his house. While he worked the land near the river, he would sometimes see boats passing by. It was this activity on the river that accounted for one of the crowning experiences of his small life.

Long ago there was a boathouse down the river from the Benson farm that rented rowboats and canoes. Sanferd was cutting hay in a nearby field one day when he heard a strange cackling coming off the river. He went down to the riverbank and saw two canoes, paddled by yellow-skinned men with slanted black eyes.

"They were talking chicken," Sanferd said. "And I was terrified. I hid in the bushes and watched them go by. I didn't know they were Japanese people. Didn't even know there was such a thing."

Once the flotilla had passed, he ran home and told his father, who explained to him the phenomenon of race. His world expanded.

Once he got started, Sanferd was a nonstop talker, but never, in all the years that I knew him, did he invite me into his house to sit down. I would always find him outside, and we would talk outdoors standing up, sometimes for two hours straight. After an hour or so my legs would begin to give out, but Sanferd would show no sign of fatigue. In fact he seemed to gain energy, talking more rapidly as time passed, layering on more stories, stringing them out one after another without prompting.

He was quieter than usual that day, so I decided to put off talking to him about the video tape, and since he was not forthcoming with his usual stories, I explained that I was headed out for a walk along the river and would see him later.

On my way back from the river I met Sanferd's nephew, Colburn, the old-car collector.

"I'm worried about Uncle," he said. "He's been staying up late at night and sleeping in his chair in the day. Sometimes he walks down to the river in the dark."

Colburn Benson was Sanferd's closest relative and his protector. Sometimes when I came to see the old man, Colburn would tell me he wasn't home or that he was asleep. Then, mysteriously, Sanferd would appear from the barn, in bright spirits, talkative as usual.

"A couple of friends of mine want to record some of your uncle's stories on video tape," I told him.

"Forget it," Colburn said. "He's too sick. We're going to have to take him to the hospital soon."

"What's wrong?"

"Just sick. He's getting old."

"No symptoms?"

"He doesn't sleep at night, and then he wants to work all day in the strawberry patch. We got to protect him. He can't be standing around telling strangers stories for some film or whatever it is. He might get sick and that would be the end. He's ninety-four."

"Well, tell him about our idea anyway. Maybe he'd like it."

"Maybe he would," Colburn said. "Maybe he wouldn't."

Across the valley that month the workers at the Digital plant would appear each morning to put the finishing touches on their building. They would swarm over the construction site, carrying heavy materials, hammering, climbing along high scaffolding, driving immense earth-moving machinery, backhoes, cranes, and bulldozers. Supervisors and engineers in short-sleeved shirts and hard hats would stand looking at large sheets of blueprints and pointing at things.

On my side of the valley things were quieter. On the twenty-sixth of August, crossing the meadow in the early evening, I noticed that the sky had turned a rich green. It seemed to merge with the forest in a uniform dome. Overhead I could see the fluttering silhouettes of feeding bats appearing and disappearing against the many shades of green. I would often see bats as I crossed the meadow at evening, but that night there seemed to be more than usual. They were everywhere, diving out of the pale heights into the darker green pools of the shaded depths just above the ground.

A colony of bats used to live in an old musty horse barn behind the house in Centreville, Maryland, where my father was born. As a boy I would make a point of going out into the backyard on summer nights to watch them. Everything seemed so lush in those summers — the sky, the green wall of the vegetation, even the air seemed colored, infused as it was with the odor of box-wood and old rose. Bats always summon up the memory of those summer nights. Whenever I crossed the meadow with my children on summer evenings the year I lived in my cottage, we would select a few stones from the ground and throw them in the air in front of the bats and watch them dive to investigate. Sometimes it would seem to me, standing there in the pale evening while my children tossed stones to the sky, that this was the way the world should be — a simple life without praise or blame, casting lures to bats on green evenings.

On that night I was alone, and rather than go into my cottage, I lay down in the grass and watched the bats course the sky. They were like porpoises of the air, gliding through the sea of the atmosphere, incessant in their passes, diving closer and closer to the ground, twisting and darting earthward, fluttering up again in silence. There was only the darkening green sky, the energetic bats, and the pulsing night chorus of the late-summer insects. But the reverie was suddenly shattered. There appeared above my head an immense bat, five times the size of the others. As soon as I spotted it, it began a deep, descending dive toward me. Just above the tree line it broke its dive, rose again, and disappeared. It took me a second or two to come to my senses and realize that this was not some immense tropical bat far out of its range but a nighthawk.

As I watched, another nighthawk appeared, and then another. One by one, in a loose formation, they moved above the clearing, dipping and lilting across the evening in a slow, lazy flight. They would keep on in this manner for days and weeks until, finally, they would come again into summer — this time in Argentina. On any evening between the twenty-second of August and the first of September from my corner of the world I could look into the sky from the ridge and see them passing; they were a part of the great breathing of the seasons, an inhalation that draws them southward each year along with their fellow travelers the shorebirds, the warblers, the thrushes and sparrows and hawks. Watching them, I realized the summer idyll was at an end.

5 The Interior River

 THE NIGHTHAWKS had disappeared from the sky above the clearing by early September. There were fewer and fewer bats, and from the long grasses and the surrounding forest the full chorus of the night-singing insects came up to pitch. Katydids whispered from the trees, and the snowy tree crickets throbbed and pulsed in the surrounding shrubbery against the background of a steady buzzing of long-horned grasshoppers, meadow crickets, and field crickets. I would go to sleep with the sound beyond the screened windows of the cottage. Sometimes at night I would wake up and hear them, and even at dawn, just before sunrise, they would still be singing, as if all the intensity of six months of growing, all the energy of the sun and the warm rains, had been channeled into insect song. They were like a blossoming crop. But their season was coming to an end.

The wheel turned. The Milky Way drifted across the sky, the summer constellations rose earlier and earlier, the Swan slowly turned her head southward; and down on earth, in the little clearing, migratory birds began to pass through. The sibilant white-throated sparrows appeared, and small, whining flocks of blackpoll warblers. I saw sharp-shinned hawks above the clearing; a few days later a flight of broadwinged hawks went over. I saw ospreys, high, circling red-tails, and once, in the field across the road below my house, I thought I saw a passing eagle.

I too became restless, and began wandering beyond the confines of my meadow. I found myself taking longer and longer walks in the woods behind my cottage. I left my ridge, crossed through the lower fields on the other side of the road, forded Beaver Brook, and climbed a hill above the highway, which separates my world from the world of Digital. On the other side of the valley of the highway, where the river of cars ran like a stiff stretch of rapids, I saw the rising Digital plant, completed now and scheduled to open in a month or so.

During the spring my brother Hugh, who lives in Rochester, New York, had been working on my father's journals. He reread and edited some three hundred pages from my father's years in China, made copies, and circulated them to various authorities on Chinese history. One day that month he brought me a fresh copy and stayed on for a few days in my cottage. He is by avocation a poet, a man at once fascinated and horrified by the metaphor of Hiroshima and Nagasaki; he once won an award for a series of poems he wrote about the experiences of a survivor of Hiroshima. One could make a case, given his obsession, that the sins of the fathers are indeed visited upon the children, since my family's connection with the events at Nagasaki is more direct than that of most American families.

While he was teaching in Shanghai, my father would regularly travel to Japan on vacation. It is clear from his journal that he came to love the country and the people; the cleanliness, the sense of order, the traditional desire for serenity impressed him deeply. One of the cities he traveled to during these visits was the Christian city of Nagasaki. He kept careful journals of these trips to Japan, and, as always in the East, he carried a camera. All his life he took pictures, but his photographs from the Orient are the most sensitive, the best composed. One of the places that he photographed during his visits was the busy working harbor of Nagasaki. Years later, on a winter afternoon in 1943 or 1944, two men in overcoats appeared at the door of our house and announced that they were from the federal government and would like to speak with my father. They retired to his study. My father closed the door, as he often did when visitors arrived, and the three of them talked for a while. It turned out that the men were from the FBI, and when they left, they took with them my father's pictures of Nagasaki harbor. It was not until August 8, 1945, that he understood why.

My brother Hugh, who happens to look very much like Abe Lincoln, has always been involved in social causes; he seems to have inherited a radical version of my father's sense of social commitment. When he was very young, he managed to absorb the idea that black people were disadvantaged, and to counteract this he would wander down to a nearby black neighborhood and distribute candy to the children. One afternoon a group of boys beat him up and took all the candy for themselves. Undeterred by such early setbacks, he went on to become a social worker. He found jobs in various settlement houses in New York until, finally, he happened on what he believed to be the segment of our society that is most discriminated against — the retarded. For twenty years now he has worked to liberate them from their infernal institutions and integrate them into society.

A visit with Hugh is a prolonged lesson in social justice. He hardly seemed to notice the way of life I had chosen for myself; he only glanced at my carefully constructed Victorian cottage with its filigree trim and its scrollwork swan, and he barely paused to admire the healthy snapdragons and cosmos in my garden. We went for walks; we ate on my terrace; we swam at the lake, but mostly we talked. We spent hours discussing my father's writing style, his life in China, his psychology, his motivation, and for one entire evening we reminisced about an extended trip we had taken one summer through the American West.

One morning I managed to get Hugh out in my kayak for an expedition on Beaver Brook. The part of the brook that we canoed snakes from Route 119 in Littleton north-northwest to a bridge over Beaver Brook Road in Westford. As the crow flies it is a distance of no more than a mile or so. As a fish swims, however, or a small boat or muskrat travels, it's a trip of three or four miles — I don't know how long exactly, never having bothered to measure the distance. Time and space tend to dissolve on the stream.

We rose early that day, wrestled my kayak through the cattails, and launched the boat into the narrow channel. Almost instantaneously the modern world seemed to fade away. Paddling among the grasses, on the flow of the amber-colored water, we could feel a palpable stillness descending. This happened to be one of those evocative autumnal days, the type of day that tends to mix memory with immediacy. There was a low mist hovering over the marshes, shot through with the raking light of the rising sun and infused with the calls of birds. The quiet pools in the backwaters were obscured; the air over the marsh was dank and warm, with a rusty, September sort of smell that was filled with promise.

Beaver Brook was created some twelve thousand years ago when an ice dam holding a glacial lake burst and the waters of the lake drained off, leaving behind a series of braided streams. In the mid-seventeenth century Europeans moved into the region and named one of these streams Beaver Brook. Partly because of the good, arable soils here, the industrial revolution that swept through this part of New England two hundred years later skipped over most of the area around Beaver Brook. Up until a few years ago, the fields, the woods, and the marshes along the stream looked pretty much as they did three or four centuries ago. There are now a few buildings in sight where roads cross the brook, and at a point just south of a narrow section of the stream that once served as a ford between two farms, there is a hideous strip of power lines. But other than that Beaver Brook is undeveloped. You set your boat in the narrow stream beside the road, give a few strokes, and you leave our time.

I have been on that section of the brook in all seasons. I skate the full course in winter when the ice is good, ski it when the snow cover is heavy, paddle through it in spring, summer, and fall, and regularly swim in it whenever the water is warm enough. But early autumn is the best time. The stream and its wildlife have grown old and comfortable then. The waters run slower and are thicker with plant life; the brook reeks in backwater sections, a thick, tropic redolence. The grasses have been cluttered with nests; the crops of young birds, of fish, reptiles, and amphibians are abundant; and everywhere the world seems lush and fruitful.

Before we had taken a dozen paddle strokes that day, we rounded a bend and surprised a family of wood ducks. They sprang into the air and went whistling off across the marshes. We saw them — or perhaps another group — about half an hour later. The wrens were chattering loudly, the red-wings were still calling, and periodically we could hear the low grunts of bullfrogs and green frogs. Mysterious splashes and squawks rose from the wet mists in the interior of the marsh, and along the banks nightshade, pond lilies, and arrowheads still bloomed.

We pushed on. Curve by curve, bend after bend we snaked through the marsh, winding through the tall grasses in some places, crossing open expanses in others, cutting close to wooded banks, only to move off again into mid-marsh. As the sun rose and the day warmed, the calls of the birds dwindled to a few idle chatters, and the frogs and the turtles and snakes emerged to feed. Great fat-bellied bullfrogs squatted resolutely on exposed clumps of mud at each bend. We saw the bright slitherings of water snakes and ribbon snakes. Painted turtles swam beneath the surface or basked on exposed logs and hummocks, and at one point, in a wide section of the brook, we saw an immense object that looked at first like a moving boulder. It was a snapping turtle — huge, primordial.

For long sections of the trip the grass was so tall we could not see over it, and contrary to everything my brother and I had been taught about small-boat handling by our boat-loving father, we stood up and sculled through the channels like gondoliers.

Beyond the wide flood plain of the brook, the banks to the south and east were wooded and as yet undeveloped. The hills ran down to the flat marshes, the marshes flowed north to the slopes of high ground, and no structure marred the view. With deep, easy strokes we sculled through this world of wrens and rushes, and every bend revealed more birds, more turtles, snakes, and frogs.

I rarely see another human being in the marshes. The few fishermen who come to the place never venture far from the nearest bridge, and canoeists have yet to discover the inner sections of the brook. But there is an old man I occasionally see. He is heavyset with patchy skin and few teeth. Each year in autumn I see his truck parked on the Great Road, and sometimes I meet him, or see him in the distance, poling along the stream. He comes to trap muskrats, and he goes about his business religiously, setting his traps and then checking them each morning. I used to spring his sets sometimes in order to give the muskrats a fighting chance, but after one or two long conversations with the man, I stopped. Vicious though his trade may be, he turned out to be the gentlest of men, simple in his outlook, a conservationist in his own way, and a man who, unlike many of the other local people, clearly appreciated the marshes.

Once in autumn I met a family of Indians in the Beaver Brook marshes. Not far from the road I saw two women and an older man standing in the shallow waters among the grasses, collecting something. I ran my boat up onto a hummock and sloshed over to talk to them. They told me that they were Wampanoags from Cape Cod and that they came up here each autumn to collect a species of grass that they could not find in their region. They would later dry the grass stems and use them in baskets. It seemed curious to me that they should travel nearly a hundred miles to collect a grass that I felt certain must grow somewhere on Cape Cod. I had studied the vegetation of the marsh, and it seemed to me the grass — it was actually a species of rush —

that they were collecting was fairly common. I suggested as much; I asked them if they could not find the grass closer to home, but they said no, only here. It was important, they explained, to gather this grass in this spot at this time of year. Only then would their baskets be good. I left them to their work, but I couldn't help wondering how they came to this obscure marsh so far from home.

My brother and I pushed on through the marsh as the sun grew hotter. I was in no hurry. I wanted to show him the essence of the place. I wanted to slow him down. The point of this trip, the meaning of this place for me, was a reordering of time so that the diurnal schedules of frogs and birds, and the slow clock of the seasons, would take precedence over the faster-paced schedules of the human world. And yet the brook has a flow. The boat was carried onward in spite of itself, and toward midafternoon, even though we had taken several long stops, we found ourselves approaching the end. We came to the set of power lines; we passed under a footbridge near a housing development and came into a section of the stream that is sometimes visited by fishermen. Slowly, as we paddled through the marsh, the outside world began to reassert itself. We heard a horse whinny from a nearby pasture; a car sounded its horn in the distance. And then I saw, washed up on a clump of reed canary grass, the essence of American civilization — an empty beer can.

As we paddled, my brother and I had been talking about Henry Thoreau and his love of the Concord River, and it occurred to me later that it was about the same time of year, early September 1839, when he was twenty-two, that Henry and his older brother, John, took their famous trip on the Concord and Merrimack rivers. Their plan was to row their home-built boat north, travel overland to the White Mountains, climb Mount Washington, and return. But what was intended originally to be a mountain-climbing expedition, in Henry's mind at least, evolved into a river journey. In his journals, and in his subsequent book (his first), *A Week on the Concord and Merrimack Rivers,* he focused on the going out and the return rather than on the far more adventurous ascent of Mount Washington. He compared the Concord River with the greatest rivers of the planet — the Mississippi, the Ganges, the Nile. Rivers were the constant lure to distant enterprise and adventure, he wrote. "Dwellers on their banks will at length accompany their current to the lowlands of the globe or explore the interior continents."

The two brothers left from Concord on August 31 and spent the night not far downstream, listening to the water sounds around them and barely sleeping in the excitement of their first night out. The next day they rowed downstream to Lowell and were locked through the city to the Merrimack River, where they turned upstream. They camped the following night near Tyngsboro, rowed northward, alternately resting and swimming, and then spent the next night beyond Nashua, New Hampshire. By Tuesday afternoon they were at the mouth of the Souhegan River, and that night they reached Bedford, where they camped by some waterfalls. They locked themselves through the manufacturing city of Manchester, bought supplies from a local farmer, and spent the next night at Hooksett. In the morning they walked to Concord, New Hampshire, and from there went overland to the White Mountains, returning to Hooksett by the twelfth of September. The rest of the voyage was downstream and, fortuitously, downwind.

The trip was a lark for the two brothers, a true vacation. They were living an experimental life; they were teaching in the decidedly untraditional school they had started in Concord; they were both in love (with the same woman); and they were, in spite of the potential for competition, good friends and confidants. John's health was questionable. He was thin, sometimes had nosebleeds that would not stop, and was often sick with what was at the time called the colic, but was in fact tuberculosis. Nevertheless, there was no reason to suspect, in the bright autumn of 1839, that in a little more than two years John would be dead.

Coincidentally, I had taken a river trip with my brother Hugh when I was twenty-two, the same age as Henry when he took his Concord and Merrimack trip. One summer a few years after he graduated from college, having got together a little money, Hugh announced that he was going out West to look around. Hugh was then a budding poet who was moved by the metaphor of America, and since I was footloose myself at that point, I accompanied him across the continent while he searched for whatever it was he was looking for. We drove out through Ohio, sleeping rough in the open air, then headed north for the Chicago stockyards, one of his favorite images from American literature. We found, upon arrival, only acre on acre of empty corrals. The butchery had moved elsewhere.

We drove on through the northern prairie, crossed the Rockies, dropped down into California, and subsequently found work in Fresno. He sold bibles; I sold Fuller brushes and worked in the lettuce fields. We grew restless, so we left, camped in the desert for a while, and then found jobs in a restaurant in Nevada, just over the California line. He pumped gas and acted as mechanic, even though he knew little or nothing about cars. I worked the night shift in the kitchen, having learned a thing or two about cooking the year before in a restaurant in France. After a few weeks we had earned enough to head south to Texas, where we had cousins.

My brother had some friends who were planning a raft trip down a section of the Rio Grande in the Big Bend area, so we drove west from Dallas and met them in a sad little restaurant in Odessa. We launched the raft at a place called Woods Landing in a near-trackless desert, having already dropped another vehicle downstream at a bridge crossing into Mexico.

For the next five days, we drifted, paddled, poled, and floated through rapids and stretches of quiet water, downstream toward the Mexican bridge. We camped each night by the side of the river, and after dinner lay on our backs staring at the sky and talking quietly. This was in the early 1960s, and at one point we saw an odd, wandering star cross the sky. It appeared over a ridge, and against the backdrop of the fixed stars moved slowly across the night until it disappeared over another ridge to our west. It took us a while to figure out that it was a satellite, the first we had ever seen. My brother, ever the cynic, suggested that it would be only a matter of time before some military use was found for the device. He went so far as to suggest that it might be used to trigger nuclear rockets.

The winter before we left for our Western trip Hugh had been studying about Hiroshima and Nagasaki, and over the spring and early summer had been working on his series of poems about the bomb. As we moved down the river, day by day he tortured us with stories about Hiroshima, read passages from his works in progress, and lectured us on the development and testing of the bomb. Moving through that desert country was like moving through a postnuclear world. The only indication that life had not ceased to exist was the river itself. The part of the Rio Grande we were on was bounded by canyons and short, steep hills. Each evening when we stopped to camp, we would climb out of the river valley and stare across a barren landscape. The world there was brown and rucked and devoid of any signs of human habitation. But snaking through this seemingly lifeless desert was the great green ribbon of the river, with its lush bank-side vegetation.

On their first night out on the Concord River, Henry and John Thoreau saw a great glow in the sky and heard, far in the distance, the clanging of fire bells. Somewhere in Lowell a fire was raging. On our first night out we climbed to a peak above the canyon walls to watch the fireball of the sun go down over the desert, and long after sunset sat there on the peak, talking. We began to descend to the river in near darkness. Halfway down the mountain, just as my brother was stepping over a rock, he heard an ominous buzzing and saw a rattlesnake, coiling itself and curving its neck back in preparation for a strike. We stepped back, then watched it for a while and let it escape, grateful to it for warning us. A year before this, on a cliff along the Palisades in New Jersey, a copperhead had struck at my brother while we were on an excursion together. It missed, and somewhat ungraciously, I thought, my brother had picked up a stick and flipped him out of our path over the edge.

On their river trip Henry and his brother stopped at local farms for milk and pie. They saw fish and muskrats, heard foxes, watched birds, and paddled and rowed through the lush watery plants that grew beside the river. My brother and I passed mile on mile of bare rock, slipped through canyons three hundred feet deep, and heard the gurgling of rock-bound water. One dawn, before first light, I heard the elegiac song of canyon wrens dropping like rainwater amidst the crevices and rock outcroppings. Hummingbirds darted above the riverside vegetation; we saw the tracks of peccaries, heard one night an odd caterwauling, watched the stars, spoke of time and history and bombs.

Three days into his trip Henry found the remnants of an ancient Indian camp near the river. Three days into our trip we found petroglyphs carved at an indeterminate time by local Indians. Henry and John locked themselves through a system of organized, channeled rivers. We came to spots in the river — well known to the river rats, as we called Hugh's friends — where we could hear ahead of us a dark roaring and gushing. Here we tied things down, approached slowly, and then swirled through rapids, skimming at one point through a narrow cut between two immense boulders which channeled the river to such a height that the raft nearly left the water entirely. We came to a quiet pool where we swam in the cold waters, and then, after a few days, came to Big Bend National Park, where we stopped at a hot spring, bathed and swam, and then, as did Henry and John, undertook a short overland trip. Henry and John went into the cool heights of the White Mountains; we went into the flat heat of the Mexican desert.

There was a small village in Mexico, not far from the Rio Grande. The river rats were dry and wanted to buy tequila *con gusano*, a favorite drink of theirs. We left the river and hiked to the town. Since I was the only one who spoke Spanish, they sent me to pick up the tequila while they drank cold beer at a local cantina. I went up the stretch of rocks and sand that served as a main road for the place, asked an old man where I could buy some wine, and went through a small, unmarked doorway up the street. It was dark inside. There was a short pine bar, and the walls behind the bar were lined with bottles and decorated with calendars showing naked women in lush, North American forest settings. It took me a minute to get used to the darkness, but once my vision cleared, I could see that the room was filled with eyes. The place was unusually quiet, but it was crowded with sad-looking men drinking in the darkness of the midafternoon. I realized suddenly that I was the cause of the silence. It was not a place that Anglos often visited, although it was only a few miles from the United States border.

I was just back from a year in Spain, and my Spanish at that time was good. As soon as I spoke, the tension was broken. It was my accent. It was clearly not Mexican, but I had lost all traces of American English, and they wanted to know where I was from, how I had gotten to their godforsaken little village, and why I had come there. They bought me a beer, and we talked about Spain, about Franco and John Kennedy and Castro, the bomb, women. A demented man kept interrupting the conversation to ask if I knew a certain tune, which he would then sing in a cackling, outlandish voice. They told me not to bother with him, and at one point gave him a warning, but he was insistent. He asked if I had a girl friend, asked me to dance, and when I politely refused, he danced by himself for a while, cackling and winking at me with his bright, crazy eyes. Someone shouted at him to dance harder, and, arms cocked on his hips, legs flying in all directions, he spun wildly around the floor until he collapsed in a chair. Someone brought him a beer, tousled his hair, and kissed him on the forehead.

I loved that bar. It was such a contrast to the wide, inhuman spaces of the desert. I had just come back from two years in Europe and I was not yet comfortable with the American landscape. The country seemed so raw to me, so huge and unfriendly and violent. Not five minutes after getting off the boat in New York I had seen a fight in the streets. The police were angry, the traffic insane, and the energy of the country, the frenetic pace of it all, had shocked me. The trip West had been a relief since my brother and I had camped alone in remote wilderness areas for much of the time. Now in Mexico I had rediscovered some of the sense of community I had experienced in southern Spain. I might have stayed there forever had the river rats not come to fetch me. The barflies and I had known each other less than an hour, but the farewells we gave there were warmer than the greetings I had gotten from some North American friends I hadn't seen in two years.

That night we were back on the river and camped in a scrape of beach below a skyscraper of a cliff, alone with the gurgle of the river and the lonely, sinking calls of the canyon wren.

The next day we drifted into a narrow canyon so deep the river was bathed in the half-light of dusk. The river rats knew this section of the Rio Grande well and instructed us to beach the boat at a little outcropping. There, above us on the Mexican side of the river, we could see a cave in the sheer face of the cliff and, dangling from the mouth, the remnants of a home-made ladder, constructed apparently from salvaged driftwood and some kind of natural fiber from a desert plant. About fifteen years earlier, according to river lore, a man had lived in the cave. The story was that when he heard that the Russians had developed the atomic bomb, he decided that nuclear war was inevitable. He became convinced that civilization was coming to an end, and he wanted to cut himself off from all human contact and spend the rest of his days in the desert. For seven years he lived alone in the cave above the river, eating rattlesnakes, lizards, and the big Rio Grande catfish. Sometimes people passing below on the river would hail him, but he would glare down at them without a word, as if they were an alien species whose chatter was incomprehensible to him. Early one spring, after a heavy downpour that raised the river and stiffened the rapids, he saw something orange washed up on the rocks below his cave. He descended to investigate and found there the body of a drowned woman. God knows what he saw in her face, but after that he gave up his isolation and returned to civilization.

When Henry and John returned to Concord after their two-week trip, the marks left in the bank by their launching were still visible. John left Concord not long after their return to visit their common love in Scituate. Henry threw himself into his work and began translating Aeschylus' *Prometheus Bound.*

When we came to the Mexican bridge we found the river rats' truck still there. My brother and I got our car and drove north, returning home in late summer. That fall Hugh went off to work in a settlement house in New York and I went on to an American college. Later that year the river rats wrote to us. They had heard that the cliff-dwelling man was selling advertising in San Francisco.

6 My Lady
of the Squirrels

JUST AFTER DAWN on the fifth of October I heard a sharp rap on the roof of my cottage, as if someone had thrown a stone. I woke up, fell asleep again, and was awakened shortly thereafter by another rap. Five minutes later I heard the noise again. I heard it the following day, and the next morning as well, and all through that week and into the following week.

It was clear by the first day what the noise was all about. Gray squirrels foraging in the hickory trees around the cottage were dropping nuts on my roof — the small stone terrace just beyond my door was littered with the shells. The work continued for the next two weeks, until they had thoroughly stripped the trees, and after a few days I became comfortable with the sound. But it was a clear sign that the cold weather was about to set in and that I had better do something about getting ready for winter.

My cottage was without insulation, without storm windows and, more to the point, without any source of heat. So early that fall I set about preparing the place for the coming season and once again found myself operating in tandem with my mentor.

Why Henry Thoreau, master of the practical arts, would wait until late autumn to begin preparing his cabin for a New England winter is beyond me, except that he seems to have enjoyed essential experiences, including the cold. It was not until November that he completed his indoor fireplace, which means he spent all of October without heat. He purchased a load of secondhand bricks and hauled up some stones and sand from the shores of Walden. He mixed the sand into his mortar, and slowly, taking his time, he layered up a good chimney and fireplace. He lathed the interior of his cabin and mixed plaster, using lime he had made himself from clamshells he had burned the winter before. He lived at his parents' house for the few weeks that it took to complete the plastering work, and then, on December 6, he moved back into the winterized summer cabin.

My work was somewhat easier. I ran an insulated chimney through a hole I cut in the roof and installed an airtight wood stove. Henry also used a stove the second winter he was at Walden, but he made do the first year with a fireplace that must have consumed wood voraciously and would have lost its fire each night, leaving the cabin cold on winter mornings. I burned good hardwood, and my stove was a small, efficiently designed European device that would burn through the night, and would sometimes hold coals for fifteen hours. Henry burned stumps that he dug up from his garden; he must have spent a good deal of his time chopping.

I thought about plastering my house, just for tradition's sake, but ended up insulating the pine walls with fiber glass and covering the interior with plasterboard. I bought more insulation for the ceiling at the local hardware store and then boarded it up with the same rough-cut pine with which I had built the walls. Henry enjoyed plastering his cottage. He went about the work slowly, and I imagine him pacing himself, listening to the call of the migrating birds in the surrounding woods as he worked and taking time off to walk and to visit with his friends in town.

By contrast I grew to hate the messy business of getting ready for winter. I do not like to measure things, and fitting the wallboard between the frames required a lot of accurate cutting. I cut the panels outdoors and brought them inside to fit, but rains plagued me, and little bits of plaster and dust began to accumulate everywhere. I am sure that I breathed in my quota of fiber-glass insulating material, and when the plasterboard was all fitted, I had to go over the walls again and do more measuring and more cutting to finish off all the trim.

Nevertheless, when I was done my cottage was snug and comfortable. I sealed all the windows, covered them with an extra set of recycled windows, puttied the cracks, and then, after the cold weather came, spent hours staring at the open door of the wood stove, enjoying the searing heat of the fire.

I had some visitors that month. A friend from the Berkshires, Alice Dart, arrived with a quiet, serious man named Randall Mason, who had spent too much time in the wilderness and had almost forgotten how to talk. The two of them were used to cramped quarters and primitive living conditions, and they were content to sleep in my loft and cook their food on my makeshift outdoor fireplace. Alice was doing research on traditional Eastern Woodland Indian basketry at Harvard, and every day the two of them would drive off to Cambridge like commuters.

One Saturday morning the three of us took a walk down to a larch swamp on the other side of some pasture land beyond the western slope of the ridge. Our intention to find black ash, a species that Alice is forever searching out in order to make basket splints. We took the trail I had made behind my house leading to the hemlock grove, and then we turned south and wandered down the west side of the ridge, climbing in and out of the hollows. On the lower slopes, about a hundred yards in from a cleared pasture, we came to a collection of immense boulders overgrown with moss and lichens, some with ferns growing on them.

Local folklore held that this site was the burial ground of some of the last Pawtucket Indians in this valley. There was a substantial Christian Indian village not far from the spot, but during King Philip's War the inhabitants of the village, their Christianity notwithstanding, were rounded up and shipped to Deer Island

in Boston Harbor, where most of them died during the hard
winter of 1676. A few stragglers returned and lived on at the
edges of civilization, reverting, some said, to their primal, sha-
manistic religion. One by one these few died off and were buried
among the boulders on the west slope of the ridge.

For some reason I was never able to find this burial site when
I set out specifically to look for it. I would come across the spot
only while I was on some other expedition. There was something
about the lay of the land, the strange south-running, short valleys
in the midst of a generally westward slope, that made that part
of the ridge hard to navigate. Sometimes, it seemed to me, different species of trees grew around the boulders at different
times; sometimes it seemed the slopes of the hollow where the
site was located angled off into different directions. The boulders
themselves were mysterious. Some were immense — twelve or
fifteen feet high — and after studying them for a while I got the
impression that there was an order to their arrangement, as if
they had been set down by Paleolithic temple builders. In fact
the arrangement was probably the work of the greatest earth
mover of them all, the glacier, and indeed, on some occasions,
staring at the rocks, I could see no order at all, simply a jumble
of broken stone.

Alice was fascinated with the spot. She had grown up in an
intensely religious household — her uncle was a well-known
Episcopalian minister — and as an adult Alice had rejected
Christianity and taken up the religions of the American Indians.
For several summers she had studied under the tutelage of a
Crow medicine woman and had spent a lot of time with various
Indian groups, learning to make baskets. One of her many the-
ories was that it was not the colonists who were responsible for
the stone walls of New England but the Native Americans.

"They used them to track astronomical events," Alice said,
"the solstices, moon rise, star positions."

She also believed that they built small temples or meditation
chambers.

"This looks just like one of their sacred spots," she said when she saw the boulders.

I told her about the burial ground, and also about a local rumor that blacks, moving north on the Underground Railroad, used to hide out among these stones.

"Slave catchers from the South used to pass through this valley. Farmers in the area who were hiding blacks would always send them out here," I told her.

"Well, that fits right in," she said. "The Indians probably guided them here. These were Pawtuckets in this area, a humane people, very spiritual."

"But the last Indian here died in 1725," I said.

"Who says?"

"The history books."

"Well, that's just our history. Indians don't believe that. They believe that they are still here. They were here in 1860 when these black people were coming through."

She looked around.

"They're still here, I bet."

Alice used to be a normal person. She used to live in a little town with tall trees in a house with a sewing room. On winter nights her mother would teach her how to stitch and cut patterns, and for years — for thirty years in fact — Alice believed that she would grow up and marry, have children, and move to a little town with tall trees. Once she did marry. Anthony Dart was a journalist who fancied himself a novelist, but who in time gave up fiction and went to work for Digital, always an option for free-lance writers in Boston. Alice was teaching art at crafts centers in Cambridge at the time, and after her husband became a computer person, she began to feel constricted by her marriage, although she wouldn't admit it to herself. The two of them managed to stay together for another year, but the year took its toll. Alice would stay up late playing the same tune over and over again on her flute. She would walk at night along the roads in Concord, and when summer came she took long, moonlit swims across Walden Pond, always alone. She grew destructive and depressed. Uncharacteristically, Anthony began to work too hard. Finally they gave up. He stayed on at Digital. She packed her draw knife, some basket materials, and a sleeping bag in her Volkswagen and headed to the Berkshires. Some friends lent her a small cabin by a pond and she settled there in September, not certain what she would do when winter came.

She used to send long, introspective letters to me and to other friends. Things were slipping. She was alone. It was autumn, and already the firewood was running low. She was nearly out of money and too proud to take any from her ex-husband. Her family was a continent away and offered no solace in any case. She was, she wrote, seemingly emptied of everything that had once filled her. "My life is flattened on the road," she said in one letter.

At night she would sit by the pond and stare into the water, listening to the call of the geese passing overhead and the lonely hoots of the owls in the nearby forest. She heard the rustling of mice, the crack of trees on windy nights. She read books, wrote more letters, studied nature, tried to find new friends. And then one night in October she looked down into the black waters of the pond and saw the sky.

The night was still and the stars were so bright that the images of the constellations were reflected on the quiet waters. She looked up and, for the first time since her childhood, saw the great band of the Milky Way arching through the night. She looked down and saw its dull glow in the waters. Water and sky seemed to merge. "The great ribbons of light formed a circle around me. And I was a part of it," she wrote. Abruptly her mood changed, the struggle eased. "I knew what it was to be reborn. I don't know what I was born into," she wrote, "but I knew I was part of this natural world."

She began to reexamine virtually all her previously held beliefs, and for the first time in her life religion seemed to make sense. The idea of a great father-god who dwelt in the sky and who had a son who was tortured to death by the very people who invented the god never made much sense to her. The existence of a spirit in trees, rocks, and animals, a sacred earth, an eternal circle of being, did. She began once again to explore the world of nature through the eyes of American Indian shamans and medicine men, and the more she studied, the more the world made sense to her. She was blond, blue-eyed, and very un-Indian in her talkative, neurotic way, but for a while she out-Indianed the Sioux and the Crow. She went to powwows, learned ritual songs and dances, built a sweat lodge for herself, and did everything but wear feathers and hunt buffalo.

None of the arts or crafts she had been involved with before had satisfied her. Except for pottery, she felt that they were removed from nature and the real world. Then as part of her immersion in Indian cultures she learned the art of natural basketry. Rather than buying materials at art-supply stores, she took to gathering them herself. She would spend days in the forest searching for suitable oak and hickory and black ash. She would locate the best trees and then return later to cut them down and strip the bark. The woods became her second home. It was this near-constant search for useful trees that led us to the ridge that day.

She was obsessed with finding black ash. "Where do we go now?" she asked me.

"On to the larch swamp," I said.

We crossed the pastures, rounded a pond at the base of the slope, and then crossed another field to the swamp. Black ash typically grows in wet areas, but search as we might, we could not find one, so we headed back, taking the route up the northern edge of the slope. The ground there is steeper and the brush thicker, and we had to struggle to walk even a few paces. Conversation fell off, and silently we picked our way through blueberry bushes and thickets of pine and scrubby oak. I thought we were heading toward the hemlock grove where we had started, but as is often the case on the ridge, we got turned around. When we broke out of the brush, we were on the old carriage road not far from the gardens at Megan Lewis' and, in fact, not that far from the boulders southwest of the grove.

In the middle of the old road Randall spotted the droppings of some large mammal. Whatever it was, it had been eating a mixture of berries and animals; we could see seeds as well as the little claws of squirrels or mice in the droppings.

"Maybe a coyote," Alice suggested.

"There are coyotes around," I said.

"But this isn't one," Randall said, breaking an hour-long silence. "This is a bear dropping."

"But there are no bears around here," I said.

"He knows his bears," Alice said, nodding.

Randall was fond of solo wilderness trips and had once spent a summer alone in Labrador. One night, Alice said, a bear had come to his camp.

"He wasn't after food," she explained. "He just sat there staring at him. Isn't that right, Randall? All night, he didn't move. No sleep, right?"

"I don't know what he wanted," Randall said.

"I do," Alice said.

"What?"

"He wanted your soul."

I told them the story of the bear that had been killed nearby in the hemlock grove, the one that had come back to life, briefly, in the form of a Pawtucket shaman.

"But that was in 1811, Alice, and no bears have been seen since," I said.

She merely smiled.

That autumn the Digital Equipment Corporation opened building number LKP 595. The building sat on the hill among a stand of white pine trees. It was a vast brick and glass structure, very angular in appearance, about ninety feet high, with long windows running the full length of the walls. On each corner, mounted on the ramparts, were TV surveillance cameras that swept to and fro across the parking lots.

Traffic increased dramatically shortly after the plant opened. At the wrong time of day it was actually possible to get caught in a traffic jam around the town square, something that used to happen only after the annual town parade on Memorial Day. Accidents were not uncommon. Once a week, it seemed, I would see shattered glass or car parts in the road.

I learned that it was possible to avoid the worst of the traffic by driving through the Digital parking lots, then on past a nearby VFW hall, with a Second World War howitzer sitting on the lawn in front. Jill Brown lived not far from LKP 595, and I took this shortcut regularly to get to her house. One day, as I was driving through the parking lot with a kayak on top of my car, one of the surveillance cameras spotted me and followed as I drove through the property, out onto the public highway, and past the lowered barrel of the howitzer.

My car is old and rusty and fairly distinctive, and I noticed that the cameras watched me on subsequent days as well. In fact, if I were more paranoid I might have imagined that the cameras and the howitzer were in communication and that some fine morning I would be blown off the road for my trespasses. But I overlooked the obvious symbolism of the juxtaposition — the marriage of war and industry — and continued to use the shortcut.

Traffic also increased beyond the common, after the Digital plant opened. Out on the Great Road the volume of the tidal bore grew substantially. On some days things would go wrong, the flow would cease altogether, and the river of cars would back up for a mile or so. This created a curious, ironic landscape, a long line of halted cars, throbbing impatiently amid corn fields and hay fields, beside fruit and vegetable stands.

There were also some changes in the human landscape of the town. In the morning, as I drove by the building, the lines of Digital workers bending up the switchback path to the plant doors reminded me of pilgrims entering a religious shrine after some long journey. Every day around noon the doors of the plant would open and the workers would stream back out. Some were model technicians complete with shiny black shoes and white socks, and the requisite shirt-pocket protector holding a neat row of pens. Some were young and health conscious, emerging, even in the colder weather, in shorts and running shoes to lap off a few miles during their lunch hour. Some practiced various methods of walking for health, striding along fanatically, eyes fixed, lifting their arms into seemingly unnatural positions. One man, a great sweating hulk, would stride along the country roads carrying dumbbells, which he would lift above his head as he walked.

Most of the workers, though, simply wandered around looking for restaurants. They always traveled in bands, little packs of men and women laughing and gesticulating, all easily identifiable as Digital workers, virtually all of them wearing, like amulets, the little plastic identification tags bearing their name, photograph, and identification number. Whatever the image, these newcomers created a stark contrast to the farm workers, shopkeepers, and housewives who for decades had constituted the daytime population of the town.

In fact, Digital workers are as varied a group as one is likely to find in industry, perhaps the freest of all the technical workers in the region. They come and go on a relaxed schedule. Freest of these, and yet, on a deeper level, the most thoroughly imprisoned, I was given to understand, were the programmers. These we did not often see on the roads on sunny days. They came and went as they pleased, when they pleased, sometimes appearing at dusk to work through the night. They were the blessed, the most fervently pious, so intent on their work that some of them were not conscious of the weather, or even the time of day. They rarely socialized with the others, but on arriving at the plant would proceed directly to their cubicles, switch on their computers, and spend the next eight to ten hours staring at the mystical light that appeared on the screen. Some would not even break to eat, while others would stay at their desks, switch off their Digital work, and play computer games while they ate.

On the other side of the valley, far removed from the isolated cubicles of these devoted monks, I stoked my wood fires, trimmed the wicks of my oil lamps, and read my journals. By night the limbs cracked above the cottage; clouds scudded past the moon, and Orion rose in silence. By day the sun angled low across the sky. Light faded early; barred shadows of the setting sun made a brindled pattern in the meadow by four in the afternoon. I dreamed of my father in China. I split wood, dressed warmly, studied Thoreau, and took long walks in the woods.

"O solitude!" Henry wrote. "Obscurity . . . I never triumph so as when I have the least success in my neighbor's eyes."

One warm day that autumn, as I was returning from the lake on my bicycle, I saw, plodding among the youthful Digital workers out on their lunch break, the dark form of an older man. He was wearing a baseball cap pulled down over his eyes, and he had on an overcoat in spite of the fact that it was an Indian summer day. In his right hand he carried a battered cardboard suitcase, held together with clothesline and electrical tape.

I knew him immediately. The winter before I built my cottage he had set up housekeeping in an island of woods created by the exit ramp between Route 2 and Route 495. Passing motorists, seeing his campfire glowing through the trees, would sometimes report him to the police. He was there even on the coldest nights. Nobody knew much about him, except that his name was Rudolph, and that he had once lived west of the area, somewhere around Leominster or Fitchburg. Prince Rudolph, as he came to be called, was like some of the old barns and outbuildings in the community: many of the local people considered him an eyesore and would have liked to be rid of him. But I enjoyed his presence. He provided a contrast to the new face of the town as he plodded along in his tattered overcoat, unshaven, with his grim mouth and angry, glaring eyes. Rudolph was not the friendly town drunk, hale and waving to passersby. He rarely looked up. Once or twice I had tried to talk to him, but he was monosyllabic.

I watched him approach the intersection at the town common. A little pack of Digital people came up from behind, moving faster; they parted around him like a wave around a piling and passed by. He didn't even glance up. I was walking my bicycle in the opposite direction, toward him, and when I was four or five feet away I greeted him. He looked up, continued on without a word, and then did a double take.

"What'd you say?" he asked.

"I said how are you?"

He seemed to contemplate this for a second or two.

"That's what I thought," he said and walked on without further comment.

7 Autumnal Tints

ONE OF THE THINGS I came to appreciate better that year was the beauty of the night sky. A few weeks after I moved into the cottage, I noticed that my night vision seemed to have improved so that I could walk up from the road on the darkest of nights without a flashlight. Sometimes I would even go for night walks to the hemlock grove, picking my way along the trail by watching the sky. The stars had never seemed so bright. I became acutely conscious of the changing position of the constellations as the seasons rolled by, and I always knew what quarter the moon was in. Some nights when I was alone in the cottage I wouldn't bother to light the lamps. I would simply sit there in the dark, watching moonlight spill in through the windows and the glass door, listening to the sounds around me.

There were three incredibly clear nights during the full moon that November. On one of those nights, when the moon was at its fullest, I sat alone in the dark for a while in front of the wood stove and then went out into the garden to watch the moon through binoculars. Many species of birds migrate at night and, although this was the end of the migratory season, every few minutes I would see a few silhouettes fly across the moon, and I could hear the sharp cry of passing shorebirds. While I was sitting in the moonlight I heard something moving around in the woods behind the wall. I stood up and saw a large dog nonchalantly shuffling through the pines. It was the size and shape of a Newfoundland. I went over to the wall and whistled for it, but it paid no attention. I whistled again and it continued on, head down, sniffing at something on the ground. I raised my binoculars, couldn't locate it, lowered them to look again, and lost the spot. The dog simply disappeared. It was very un-doglike in its behavior, and curiously indifferent to my presence.

My children and I had a number of little adventures with the wildlife of the ridge that autumn. One Saturday morning in early November my son, Clayton, was digging a hole in my new garden at the southwest corner of the stone walls that surround the meadow. As he was working he had a sense that something was watching him, looked up, and saw on the other side of the wall, staring at him with its golden eyes, a full-grown Eastern coyote.

The animal was about ten yards back in the woods, standing with its mouth slightly open and its ears pointed sharply forward. Clayton thought at first that it was a strange-looking dog, but he quickly realized from its markings that it was a coyote. For a few seconds the two of them stared at each other across the wall, then Clayton began to back away through the garden while the coyote watched him steadily, apparently unafraid. By the time I got to the garden, it had disappeared.

One morning my daughter, Lelia, left the cottage to catch the school bus and returned in tears. She had surprised a herd of deer feeding in the meadow, and when they saw her they had "charged" her, she said, their great autumnal antlers lowered. Some weeks later I saw another coyote drift across the clearing, a shadowy, ghostlike form that loped through the grasses as if it were moving a few feet above the ground. It was a misty gray day, and the coyote seemed to materialize from the mist, cross the open ground, and disappear into the mist again. On a warm day that same month, while I was reading in the garden, a young fox climbed over the wall and curled up in the sun at the south-west corner of the meadow and promptly fell asleep, unconscious of the fact that I was sitting no more than twenty yards away.

The squirrels continued to feed in the oak and hickory trees in the nearby woods throughout that month. The remnant leaves shuddered and fell, and the stark, bare bones of the forest revealed themselves for the first time since April. Rains came — long, soft days of mists and leaden skies. The weather cleared, there was another Indian summer, and then, abruptly one morning, great racks of winter clouds scudded across the skies bearing a front of winter cold. Orion rose earlier and earlier each evening; sparrows filtered through the dried flower stalks in my garden. Immense flocks of high-flying Canada geese moved overhead. I stoked my wood fires, made tea, and embarked on a project to reread the old classics. I read *Treasure Island, Alice in Wonderland,* and *Wind in the Willows* to my children; *The Iliad, The Odyssey, Gilgamesh,* and *Beowulf* I read to myself. The cottage was snug and warm and silent, a fine retreat from the twentieth century.

Unlike Henry Thoreau, who made do with only a few books, I had moved into my cottage a small library. I lined my walls with shelves, and as they filled, I built more. The little cottage was getting crowded. I salvaged some old family teapots. I collected more photographs and mementos from my father's years in the Orient. Sometimes when I was alone I would take down the mysterious figurine of the man with the bowl and inspect it in the gleam of the fire from the wood stove. And sometimes I would play long, slow fugues on the old parlor organ against the west wall.

This organ was a fine piece of carpentry. It was built sometime around 1890 — about the time my father was born — and it had a remarkably clear tone and many working stops. I would start quietly enough, on those still evenings, but in time, line by line, the music would consume me and I would find myself pumping harder and harder, pulling out the stops one by one to layer on harmonies until, finally, I would snap out the great subbass and let the dark bass lines roll outward. I have no formal training in music, but since childhood I have been able to improvise on various instruments, and sometimes at night in the cottage it seemed that it was not me playing but some other, more talented soul who had temporarily moved into my body and actually *knew* how to construct music rather than pretend. Anyone passing in the nearby woods, hearing those wild fugues pouring out from the dimly lit cottage, would no doubt have avoided the place, presuming that a madman lived there. I would occasionally lose track of time while I was playing and would stop only when my fingers were too tired. Then, in the silence that followed, it seemed to me that the cottage would settle to earth, as if it had been floating above the ground.

Beyond the house the world grew somber as winter advanced. Inside it was warm and softly lit with the golden glow of the oil lamps. Over the stove I hung bunches of herbs I had grown that summer in the garden. I put flannel sheets on the beds, unpacked wool blankets, split wood by day, and listened to the high bark of passing wild geese by night. I imagined that I could give away all my money and live happily on nothing, and I began to suspect, as I had all along, that this Henry Thoreau, for all his nasty griping at the world of human affairs, was right.

By November the pattern of my life in the cottage had changed because of the onset of cold weather. Every morning I would shake down the stove, make coffee, bank the fire, and then sit and read or write by the stove for a while before leaving for work. When I returned at night I would stoke the fire again before dinner. Frequently I would not bother with the tiresome work of lighting the lamps and would sit there by the glow of the coals waiting for the log to catch, listening to the warm crack of the growing fire. Occasionally, on very cold days when the fire had burned low, I would pour myself a glass of Russian vodka and drink it neat to take the chill off. Hardly a serious drinker, I would sometimes emerge into the sharp autumnal night gloriously drunk, either with the vodka or with the beauty of the cold autumn sky. My mentor would have been appalled by this custom, but then poor old Henry — never to taste the sharp fire, and never to have known the glory of hot tea or coffee.

I would eat dinner with my children and then return to the cottage with one or both for the night. After they went to sleep in the loft, I would stay up reading my various journals. And in this manner, day by day, during the week I would lead the quiet, small life of a peaceful student of the world.

On weekends I would desert my spartan existence and go out to restaurants or concerts or the ballet in Boston or Cambridge, only to return through the dark rural landscape to the black sky of the ridge. That winter I rekindled an interest in music, lectures, drama, and opera, which I had enjoyed in the years when I lived in New York, and it seemed to me that I was somehow slipping backward toward youth instead of growing old and complacent as we are supposed to.

In spite of — or maybe because of — my primitive living conditions, I considered myself well-off. Sometimes at night, returning from Boston, with the temperature dipping well below the freezing mark, I would see the glow of Rudolph's fire in the island of woods by the exit ramp of the highway. On other days I would spot him plodding along, his head bowed against the wind. Once I saw him resting in the sun on the steps of the hardware store in the town. I tried again to strike up a conversation.

"Cops get you the other night?" I asked. I had seen a police cruiser parked near his campsite.

"Just the state boys," he muttered. "Curious sons of bitches."

He looked away to avoid further discussion, and I moved on. Rudolph was known to the local police. The winter before on bitterly cold nights they had been in the habit of stopping by his camp to see if he would prefer to spend the night in jail, where it was warm. "No thanks," he would reply. "Too hot."

"Well, good luck," I said, and walked on, not wishing to intrude on his thoughts.

*

I saw my friend Emil at the hardware store that month. He was dressed, as always, in baggy corduroys, a heavy sweater, and sandals over thick wool socks.

"But we never see you anymore," he said, shaking my hand, as he always did, even if we had seen each other the day before.

"Work," I said. "I've built this cottage on my land. You should come and see it."

"Yes, yes, but we must take a walk in the woods this month. It is not too late. The oaks have held their leaves." Emil was from Austria and spoke a beautiful English that he had learned in Britain in the 1930s. He and his sister, Minna, lived in a small house they had built in a clearing just south of the lake on the other side of the ridge. They grew most of their food; they had extensive vegetable and herb gardens, a small herd of goats, a flock of chickens, and hives of bees, and they collected most of the fuel for cooking and heating from their own carefully maintained wood lot, a marvel of forest management, with neatly trimmed hardwoods and not a hint of brush or deadwood on the forest floor. I had met them through Higgins, who made a point of knowing all the interesting or eccentric people within a fifty-mile radius. When I first moved to the area, he and I would walk through the woods to Minna and Emil's on Sunday afternoons to talk and drink their homemade wine.

Every time I would see Emil or Minna, we would plan a walk or a canoe trip on one of the local rivers. Somehow, though, these expeditions never seemed to develop. They were always too busy with one or another of their various homesteading projects.

"Higgins and I will come over this Sunday, perhaps," I said. "We can talk and make plans."

Higgins and I showed up as promised on Sunday afternoon, a clear, brilliant November day with oak leaves hanging in little clusters throughout the forest.

This was the first time I had been to Emil's since I built my cottage, and seeing the place again, I realized the influence this house had had on my building notions. It was small, maybe 1,400 square feet, with gable ends built from local granite and a long row of salvaged windows crossing the south side. It was of heavy post-and-beam construction, with a single, large downstairs room that served as kitchen, dining room, and living room. A ladder on the north face led up to the second floor, where the family had their bedrooms. There was a handsome enamel wood stove in the center of the downstairs room and next to it, near the alcove that served as the kitchen, a long wooden table. Emil and Minna greeted Higgins and me effusively, as they always did. I don't believe they had many visitors. In fact, I think Higgins and I were almost their only friends. Minna had three grown children, one or two of whom were often visiting, and sometimes when we went there the whole family would gather at the door to shake our hands or embrace and kiss us repeatedly. On this day, however, Emil and Minna were alone, and after the requisite number of handshakes, kisses, and embraces, we settled down to discuss life. Emil seated us at the long table and took out a bottle of homemade May wine from an oak cabinet. Minna set out glasses, placing one in front of each of us. Emil poured the wine, catching the drips with a white dish towel as he topped off the glasses.

"Drink," he said, "to November and the harvest home."

"To November," we chanted.

I knew Emil better than any of the others in the family since he was the one I would most often encounter away from their house — he was the official errand runner, and often he would walk on the ridge looking for mushrooms. Whenever I saw him we would talk for nearly an hour, even though he would announce every five minutes or so that he had to move on. Over the years, through these various bits of conversation, I had pieced together his story.

The family had lived a fairly substantial middle-class life in Vienna in the 1930s. Emil was a set designer; Minna was married and starting a family. Minna's husband, who was a Jew, went underground and disappeared after the Nazis took over. Emil joined an antifascist group, and early on in the war was captured and sent to a prison camp in Czechoslovakia, where he worked in the mines as a slave laborer. He lived on ersatz coffee, bread made mostly with sawdust, and soup consisting of water in which the greens and vegetables for the guards had been cooked. After some months in the mines he managed to get an office job. He was good at languages and he was friendly and persuasive — he told me once he even came to like his prison-camp boss and had actually visited him in Berlin after the war.

The office job gave Emil access to a typewriter, paper, and forms, with which he forged, probably with his boss's knowledge, a weekend pass. He got in the habit of leaving the camp early on Saturday morning to walk in the villages and mountains, and soon began staying out all night when the weather was warm, and sometimes even when it wasn't. He began to live off the land. He learned all the edible wild plants in the mountains and would graze the slopes like a goat. Mushrooms were abundant in autumn; he would eat greens in spring, tubers and roots in summer and fall. In winter he would make tea with twigs or pine tips, or beg food from local cafés and farmhouses. He fashioned a pair of skis so he could travel through the mountains in the winter. One day, he told me, he ascended higher than usual, crossed a valley he had not seen before, and came to a small house in a high pasture in a district different from the one in which the prison camp was located. He knocked on the door, thinking to ask for a bowl of milk. A woman about his age opened the door, realized he was a prisoner, and told him she had nothing to give. He recognized her as a German, and made it clear that he was on some official mission and was headed back to his camp. As he was leaving, she nodded him inside and then fed him a full meal of meat, potatoes, and turnips. He ate in silence and left.

"Not a word of this, you understand?" she said to him as he went out the door. "But come back. I will feed you."

He visited her the next weekend, and the next, and throughout that winter, eating better and better each time. She explained later that she was the wife of a German officer who had been sent to the Russian front. She had not heard from him since early October. Emil related all this to me, without a wink, without any suggestion that there had been anything sexual between them, only this weekly exchange of food. In prison, he said, nourishment was his consuming passion.

"So, is this a good year for you?" Higgins asked.

"Not bad at all," Emil said. "Rain for all of April, of course, as always here. We are low here, Higgins, as you know; this is bottom land, near the lake. So we raise the beds — then we are dry, eh? Not bad, Higgins."

"Not bad at all; we are having good greens this year," Minna said. "Except for these dogs; they are taking chickens. I have seen this one, very ugly, like a police dog, but terrified if it sees you."

"We are going to have to do something," Emil said.

"We don't like to do it," Minna said. "But he is eating three, maybe four hens now."

"What will you do? Kill it?" I asked.

They seemed embarrassed by this and merely nodded sadly and changed the subject.

"I've seen a weird dog," I said. "An immense thing with shaggy fur and a round back. No interest in people, though, and it is very fast."

"Big?" Minna asked.

"Yes; black, I think."

"I've seen this fellow in the woods. He must belong to the farm. But he's not a bad sort, I don't think — too lazy. It's this police dog we dislike."

Minna was looking better than I remembered. She seemed to

have fleshed out a little, and she had let her hair grow. Unlike
Emil, who still dressed like a European, she always wore American jeans and flannel shirts. So did her three children. The two
sons were living in Amherst, and her daughter, Ursula, was in
Boston, but they would come back regularly to help with the
goats or to collect the honey from the hives. In spite of earlier
deprivation the family was very healthy; they lived well on what
little money Emil earned by teaching languages and set design.
The one anomaly in their healthy lives, other than a taste for
homemade wine and strong coffee, was an addiction to white
sugar. Emil would heap spoonfuls of it into his coffee, and they
kept a great silver bowl in the middle of the table mounded with
white granules, which rose like a snowy mountain above the
edges of the bowl.

One of their favorite subjects was their own way of life. Higgins
was a fellow traveler of theirs; of all the people in the community,
he and Jane were most like Emil and Minna. Nevertheless Emil
seemed to think Higgins needed conversion, and whenever we
were there the whole family would launch into praises of the
good life, for Higgins' sake.

"You see this, Higgins?" Minna would say, waving her arm
back toward the kitchen alcove, with its braids of onions and
garlic and its shelves of homemade preserves. "All this we grow."

"You drink this wine, Higgins? You drink summer light. This
is good."

"I understand," Higgins would say.

They would interrupt before he could continue.

"This is the good life, Higgins. We go into the forest and we
cut our fuel. We go to the hen house, and every morning — new
eggs. This earth grows for you."

"The good bounty, Higgins," Minna said.

"The good earth," Emil echoed.

Ironically, considering the abuse they had taken at the hands
of Germans, they loved Wagnerian opera. Sometimes they would
make us listen with them in silence while they played us their

favorite passages. That day they wanted us to hear something from *Tristan und Isolde*. Emil rose, put a record on the stereo, returned to the table, and sat down, nodding his head contemplatively, waiting for the passage he wanted us to hear. Minna had closed her eyes.

"Now, hear this," Emil said. One of the leitmotifs emerged from the dark music, barely perceptible unless you knew what to listen for. They closed their eyes and listened, quiet for once, occasionally lifting their hands at significant passages or even toasting silently with their wine glasses, and waving their heads slowly to the flow of the music.

"Beautiful, is it not, Higgins?" Emil said after the piece was over. "How can you deny that this is the pinnacle of human endeavor?"

Higgins did not like opera and they knew it.

They put the leitmotif on again.

Higgins rolled his eyes at me, but I was enjoying the moment. They had left the front door open, and the fresh air of November was spilling into the room. At one point a little flock of sparrows flitted past the open door, feeding on the tomato vines that still clung to the wall of the house.

"To Richard Wagner," Emil said, lifting his glass.

"To Wagner," I repeated.

We drained our glasses.

They launched into another litany of things that were good and also free. These litanies often began with a toast, but would soon assume a life of their own.

"Sun," they said. "The sun is free."

"Fresh air."

"The sky."

"Rain."

"Soil."

"Birds. Bird song is free."

"Love of nature."

"Wagner," I said, joining the praises.

"Yes, yes, Wagner is free," Minna said.

"Not really," Higgins said. "You have to be rich to hear Wagner. You have to pay to go to the opera. You have to pay for the stereo or the electricity."

"Well, Wagner should be free. It is the fault of the state. It is the problem with this world," Minna said. "You can't have good things by the state. Only the bad. The guns and the bombs."

"But here we live without the state," Emil said. "Minimal at least. We do not see police here." He winked at me.

"Here is only the gardens and the chickens, and the wind at night," said Minna. "This is free, Higgins. The wind — no state can control it."

"Do you vote?" I asked.

"Yes, we vote," Minna said. "But after that, what? You get the same. Maybe that is a good thing. But always we are working in spite of the state."

Minna was part of a peace group that for years used to hold a vigil every Saturday morning on the town common. It was her one social activity.

"This is here the minimal state," she said. "I go to the common every Saturday to say to the world that this is the minimal state. That you can stand outside with others and say that the state is not good. Higgins, I have seen the state at its worst. No one in this world has seen the state as I have. It is a thin line, this government."

"So we stay here," Emil said. "We stay here and grow vegetables and keep to ourselves."

"But next time we will fight," Minna said.

"Or retire farther to wilderness. We are old."

"No, I will fight," Minna said.

"I will fight, too," Higgins said, standing up.

"Someday, Emil, you and Minna should come down with me to Walden Pond to visit the site where Henry Thoreau once lived. He went to jail to protest an immoral war."

"To Henry Thoreau, man of peace," Higgins said.

"I drink," Emil said. Even though they were among the most Thoreauvian individuals I knew, they did not know much about Henry.

"To Henry," I said.

"To life without the state," Minna said.

The May wine was beginning to assert itself. We toasted the good life again. Emil toasted the soil. We toasted autumn, and the harvest, and world peace, and when we finally rose to go, they clustered around us at the door. We shook hands heartily, we embraced, we kissed. We shook hands again, and then Higgins and I wandered up the hill away from the house, their farewells still echoing through the darkening November woods.

I went up to Walden Pond more often than usual that autumn. I was reading Henry's journals for November, and I got into the habit of visiting some places he mentioned to see what changes had occurred. In spite of the controversy in our time over the use of the pond, it was one of the places that had changed the least, and it was particularly pleasant in autumn. The summer crowds were gone, the winter ice fishermen had yet to arrive, and I was alone with the walkers and the few tourists who would come to see the pond. I would wander down to Thoreau's cabin site on the northwest side of Walden, far from the road, and whenever I spent any length of time there I would almost always meet other pilgrims.

Once I saw a man in a maroon robe making his way through the forest with a little group of people around him. He turned out to be an eminent Tibetan monk, a student of Thoreau, who was visiting New York and had made a pilgrimage to Concord to visit the site of Thoreau's cabin. Another day that November I met at the cabin site a well-dressed man of about forty who was a lawyer from New York City; he looked very tired. He and I fell into conversation, as often happened when I met visitors at the site, and he explained that twice a year, sometimes more often, he would come to this spot to put the world in perspective.

"You've got to understand," he explained, "I live twenty floors up, a closed-in world. By day I travel down an elevator, walk three hundred and eight steps to a subway, emerge into the light, walk exactly five hundred and four steps to a subway, emerge into the light, walk exactly five hundred and twenty-nine steps to a door, and enter into my office building for the next eight to ten hours. At night I read Thoreau. I read a few lines and daydream. Read a few more and dream some more. It's a way of traveling. And sometimes I come here, just to make sure it's all real."

One day at the pond I met a woman who was a member of the Libertarian party. She claimed, perhaps with some justification, that Thoreau was the patron saint of libertarianism.

"He was the first anarchist in the best sense of the word," she said. "No rules need apply. Each to his or her own. And I agree."

I met a Catholic priest at the pond one day who said that he believed Thoreau was a deeply religious man even though he never attended church. "He was a catholic in the original sense of the word — that is to say, he was universal in his thinking, accepting all paths."

Once I met a man in a headband wearing a fringed deerskin jacket. He said he was part Cherokee and that Thoreau was the only white man in nineteenth-century America who understood the native American. "All his life Henry collected information on Indians. He lived like an Indian. He should have been born four hundred years earlier in Concord. People then wouldn't have thought he was so weird. He was a man out of his time. That's all."

One Saturday I went to Walden with a band of people led by Roland Robbins, the man who, in the 1940s, had discovered the site of Thoreau's cabin. Most of the ten or twelve people with Roland were devoted Thoreauvians of one sort or another, and when we reached the house site we found other pilgrims there, trooping through the oaks and pines as to a religious shrine. Some of them carried stones they had brought from other parts of the globe. They placed the stones on a cairn near the house site in memory of the man who had lived there, following a tradition that had begun at this spot in the late nineteenth century. Once, years ago, the state had declared the cairn an eyesore. Backhoes came and hauled away the rocks. But day by day they began to reappear, and in the end the authorities gave up. The mound of stones is now some ten yards across and about three or four feet high.

By November of 1845 Henry Thoreau had been living at Walden Pond for four months. The fogs of autumn had come, the leaves had been stripped from the trees, and the woods around him had turned a somber brown. Waterfowl began to appear in the skies above the pond and over the river to the west of his cabin. Black ducks and teal whistled by, and he heard the clamor of a solitary goose circling through the fog, "seeking its mate," as he wrote. Hunters appeared at the pond and along the river, and for hours that fall Henry watched the swimming ducks tack back and forth in little flocks, keeping in the middle of Walden Pond, away from the range of the guns. A loon dropped into the pond, laughing and whinnying. Henry studied it, recorded its behavior, and subsequently wrote about it in *Walden.* He kept his journal, and as always he read deeply. He delved into Carlyle, he studied Ariosto, read his Homer and Aeschylus and Hallam's history of the literature of Europe, which inspired him to read *Abelard and Heloise,* Pulci's *Morgante Maggiore,* and Boiardo's *Orlando innamorato.*

He was Henry the inscrutable — the practical man who made his own lime, plastered his own cottage walls, and cut his own firewood; the scholar who filled his notebooks with ideas and thoughts on his readings; the journal writer who kept track of squirrels and snowstorms and examined the lives of the human inhabitants of his woodland, the Irish shantymen, the French-Canadian woodcutter Therien, and the escaped slaves who passed through Concord. Henry was forever the enigma, the naturalist, the loner, the acerbic dinner guest, the friend of children, the foe of the established. He did not pay his poll tax; he did not join the church; he did not even join the various transcendental communities his friends belonged to. And he was, finally, Henry the bachelor, the unmarried man.

Bachelorhood was perhaps not much of an issue in the nineteenth century, but twentieth-century man that I am, I could not help finding this aspect of Henry's life mysterious. Although he had many women friends and confided in them readily, it appears that he never developed a long-standing, intimate relationship with a woman. And yet he did propose marriage once, although, curiously enough, the woman to whom he chose to offer his hand was his brother's girl friend, as if marriage should be kept within the immediate family; and he was nothing if not a good family man, loyal to the end. In fact, he never really left home.

In the summer of 1839 Ellen Sewall came into Concord, the daughter of Edmund Sewall, whose son had been attending the Thoreau brothers' school and living at the Thoreaus' boarding-house. Photographs of Ellen Sewall show a serene, half-smiling, contented woman with intelligent eyes and a strong, beautiful face. She was soon the center of attention at parties and the object of the affection of at least one other unattached gentleman in the village. But the Thoreau brothers took up most of her time. The three of them went boating together; they took walks; they went berrying and riding. Henry took Ellen to see a giraffe that had been brought to Concord by a touring circus. He also took her out alone in his boat. In fact the only thing he would not consent to do with her was go to church. She asked him to accompany her one day and, even though by this time it was clear that he was falling in love with her and would welcome almost any excuse to be near her, he refused. He knew where his priorities lay.

Ellen was in town for a mere two weeks that summer — the same summer Henry and John went on their trip on the Concord and Merrimack rivers. Just after they got back, John went off to Scituate to visit Ellen; Henry stayed home. John's visit was a success, and it appeared that he had gained the upper hand in the courtship. Henry wrote obscure passages about love in his journal, but there was no hint of jealousy or anger toward his beloved brother.

At Christmas that same year John went off again to visit Ellen in Scituate. Henry went with him this time and, on returning, to Concord, the brothers matched each other with letters and gifts. John sent her opals and books. Henry sent poems. He also sent her a lecture against tea and coffee.

Ellen came back to Concord the next summer, 1840, and Henry again managed to take her rowing alone. He recorded the incident in his journal on June 19. It was a lovely day. Ellen sat in the stern, and Henry sat amidships, facing her. Her figure broke into the line of the sky, creating a beautiful image. "So might our lives be picturesque," Henry wrote.

There was heat lightning that night. In the streets the lowing of the cows seemed to Henry to have a friendly, comfortable aspect. The voice of the whippoorwill drifted across the fields and mingled with the sounds of the cows. The woods and moonlight wooed him. Henry Thoreau was in love.

But John, three years older and the more sociable of the two, went back to Scituate for a visit, accompanied, as always, by Ellen's watchful Aunt Prudence, who was also a boarder at the Thoreaus'. They walked the beach one day; by good fortune Aunt Prudence became tired and sat down on a rock to rest. As soon as they were out of earshot, John began to plead his case. He asked Ellen to marry him, and somewhat taken aback, she accepted. They returned to the house, but after talking to her mother, Ellen realized she had made a mistake. She told John she had changed her mind. Ellen's father was a Unitarian minister, and the Thoreau brothers were known transcendentalists and far too extreme in their views for her father to be comfortable with either of them.

Some Thoreau scholars have suggested that Ellen actually

loved Henry, not John. Some have suggested that she truly loved John but could not defy her father's will. Whatever the case, back in Concord, Henry seemed elated. "The night is spangled with fresh stars," he wrote, meaning, some believe, that he knew of Ellen's rejection and thought that the way was cleared for him.

Henry wrote her a letter proposing marriage. He made a draft of it in his journal and there spoke of the "sun of our love." But Ellen wrote her father telling him of the proposal and was advised — ordered perhaps — to write "Mr. Thoreau" a short, explicit, and cold letter telling him that she could not marry him.

The romance was over. It was November. The ducks swept across the wintering skies, the guns of hunters sounded. The woods grew somber, the blue waters of Walden Pond turned gray. He slept alone and would forever.

8 The Green Man

AT DAWN on the tenth of December a stag crossed the meadow below my cottage and disappeared into the woods beyond the wall.

It had first snowed that year in late November, a light dusting that lingered in the shaded corners and brought up the color in the lion-brown grasses, the stone walls, and the bark of the hickories. Another snow came a few days later, a heavier one that covered the meadow and the woodland floor. Little flocks of sparrows and juncos passed through, feeding on the exposed weed stalks that still remained above the snow. Then the rains returned, a slow misty drizzle, and after that a cold spell that froze the world into a long sheet of thin ice.

I was up before dawn on the tenth, daydreaming at the window, when I heard the crash of breaking ice in the woods. I looked up just in time to see a full-grown buck with a great rack of antlers clear the wall on the east side of my land, bound across the meadow, and effortlessly sail over the stone wall on the southwest side of the clearing. It was moving fast, but I could see its rich brown eyes and its woods-colored coat and thick, healthy fur. I opened the door and went out onto my terrace. I could hear more noise from the old field north of my property, and I saw two large dogs there, tongues lolling and noses to the ground.

These might have been someone's pets, but here, in the icy December forest, they had been transformed into primitive hunting canines, recent memories of warm houses and rugs extinguished within them. They were both mongrels, thick-furred and heavily infused with the genes of German shepherd, very wolflike in appearance, and far larger and more dangerous looking than the coyotes I had seen in the area. Without thinking I grabbed a stick, placed myself in their path, and shouted at them. They pulled up abruptly, stared at me for a second or two, and then turned tail and ran.

On certain days on the ridge it would seem to me that the normal direction of the flow of time had gotten stalled out, or run backward, or become confused. This was one of those days. Everything that morning seemed brown and wild — the deer, the landscape, the dogs, the icy, snow-covered meadow, and the misty woodland sky. Just after the deer disappeared into the woods, a group of crows that had been roosting in the trees beyond the wall rose and flew out over the clearing, cawing. They settled on some exposed branches not far from me. Except for the dogs it was a vision of primitive America.

The air was still, the traffic of the nearby commuters was quiet, and I seemed to be alone on the ridge a thousand miles from civilization. I walked back toward the hemlock grove following the walls constructed here by some forgotten landholder in the years when all was orchard on the hill, save for the hemlock stand. Just southwest of the hemlocks was the Indian burial ground where the last of the Pawtucket people lay. Residents of the town used to say that a few of the Indians refused to give up even after they were dead and buried, and that one in particular continued to plague the colonial farmers along the ridge in the late eighteenth and early nineteenth centuries. He used to steal fruit and raid barns. Sometimes farmers would see him, spear in hand, standing naked at the edge of a field. On one occasion the locals organized a manhunt to catch him, but he disappeared into the thickets in one of the hollows and they couldn't root him out. His raids became fewer and fewer after the manhunt, and by the middle of the nineteenth century, when apple growing was at its height in the valley around the ridge, he disappeared for good.

A wall separates my land from the land that belongs to the farmer who lives over the hill. That still morning, just beyond that wall, barely visible on the sheet of ice, I saw what I thought was a human footprint. There was another a few feet beyond. I stepped forward and broke through the ice, took a few more steps following the track, breaking through each time I moved. The prints were not very clear. They were the size of a human foot, but they seemed slightly wider, and the trail was erratic. They would turn left or right, zigzag oddly, circle back, and then continue on toward the hemlock grove. They seemed to disappear completely at one point, and I figured I had lost them. But then fifty yards farther on I saw them again. They entered the hemlock grove and then disappeared altogether.

I went under the trees and stood there for a few minutes. The crows that had gathered when the stag crossed the clearing began calling loudly again just outside the hemlocks, cawing periodically and making deep croaking noises. The resident porcupine was back. I could see its droppings and a few quills under one of the hemlocks, and high up in the trees the rounded shape of its body. It had spent last winter in a single large tree in the grove and now it had returned. A squirrel materialized out of one of the nearby oak trees and dashed wildly across the canopy of the forest. A little flight of chickadees and titmice moved through the woods. I heard a flock of winter finches go by above the trees. Other than these natural passages of a winter day the grove was empty. And yet I felt there was something nearby. I went back and looked at the footprints outside the stand of hemlocks. The tracks were barely perceptible, and, unless they had been made when the ice crust was thicker, whoever made them should have broken through the ice. I was getting cold in the woods, and it was clear that whatever had made the tracks was not going to reveal itself to me that day, so I went back to my cottage, put another log in the wood stove, and made some more coffee.

I had been reading my father's journal that morning, and I was thinking about him while I was in the hemlocks. He was something of a trickster and had a number of routines that my friends and I used to enjoy. One was his Dr. Jekyll and Mr. Hyde act, in which he would approach with his hand extended in greeting and then spin around, ram the brim of his hat down, and reappear as Mr. Hyde, snarling and growling, his fingers crooked like claws. Even though I had seen this trick many times, I was always a little shocked, frightened even, by the horrific energy of Mr. Hyde and my father's ability to transform himself so thoroughly.

Another one of his tricks involved bears. He had learned to make an exact replica of a bear track in sand or soft soil by dragging the palm of his hand backward a few inches and then making the indentation of claws with his fingers. Once he terrorized one of his city friends who was visiting us at a summer place we had on a lake in northern Vermont. My father forged bear tracks on a sandy beach on the other side of the lake, and later he brought his friend to the spot in the canoe and "discovered" the tracks. He went off to look for the bear, leaving the poor man shaking in the canoe. Then my father set up a horrid growling in the woods, raced out of the forest, and pushed off in the canoe as if the bear were hot on his tracks.

This transformation from man to bear was not so far-fetched. The Eastern Woodland Indians used to say that the bear was their instructor and guide, a half-human intermediary between the spirit world and the world of human affairs. A thousand years ago, according to Pawtucket legend, there dwelt on the ridge behind my cottage a shaman who could change at will from bear to man. The local folklore of the Yankee farmers who supplanted the Pawtuckets holds that it was this being who was killed in the hemlock grove behind my house in 1811.

Such legends made me wonder, of course, about the origin of the curious footprints. But there were other explanations, perhaps more likely. The most logical was that Prince Rudolph had been around. Of all the people in the community, save the hunters who would patrol the meadows along Beaver Brook, he was the only one who spent any time in the forest. Furthermore, I had not seen Rudolph's fire in a few weeks, and, since the ridge was one of the last large undeveloped tracts in the town, it would not have been surprising if he had set up camp nearby. I had begun to feel a certain communion with Rudolph with the onset of winter. Living close to the edge of cold myself, I had come to appreciate the precarious nature of his existence.

A week or so after he disappeared from the exit-ramp site where he usually camped, I went to the police station to ask about him. The dispatcher at the desk was suspicious and wanted to know the purpose of my visit. Before he would tell me anything, I had to give my name, address, reason for inquiry, occupation.

"You his lawyer?" he asked.

"No, I'm just curious."

"What are you, his lawyer?" he repeated.

"No," I said.

"What do you want to know about him for?"

I began to worry that something nasty had happened to Rudolph. "Is he all right?" I asked.

"What are you, a relative or something?"

"No, I'm just curious about him. I haven't seen him around in a few weeks. Is he all right?"

"So why are you curious?"

I caught the drift and gave the answer he wanted. "I'm a journalist doing a story for the *Christian Science Monitor* on the homeless," I said. It seemed to satisfy him.

Another policeman was standing behind the desk. The dispatcher turned and repeated my occupation. The policeman nodded.

"Wants to know about that bum by the highway," the dispatcher said.

The policeman was an easygoing, heavyset man whom I had seen around town.

"He's all right. Someone saw him out on Route 2 yesterday," the policeman said.

"He's all right," the dispatcher said, "they seen him on the highway."

"I was just wondering about the rain and snow we've been having, how he gets by."

"He wants to know about the rain," the dispatcher said. He didn't seem to like the fact that the policeman was speaking to me directly.

"He gets by," the policeman explained. "He's a real loner, though. Won't even come into jail on bad nights. He always tells us to get lost when we stop by to check on him."

The dispatcher nodded authoritatively and remained silent, glaring.

Rudolph was not the only person who might have left tracks in the grove. It was possible that the Green Man had returned. I had first moved to the ridge in the early 1970s, when my wife and I had found a run-down farmhouse on the lower slope on the eastern side. The area had been even more deserted then than it was when I built my cottage several years later. The single road that crossed the eastern edge of the slope was narrow and rutted and had very little traffic; you could lie down on it at midday without danger. Two of the farms along the road were still working, and there were a number of deserted barns and houses. In the first week after I moved in I got into the habit of taking long walks through the fields and woods. Sometimes I went in search of mushrooms, sometimes in search of birds or plants, but mostly I went just to walk — simply to explore the empty forest. After a few months of this exploration I came to know the ridge; I got to know all the little secret hollows and sunny hillsides and even the individual trees. I began ranging farther and farther afield, and sometimes I would allow myself to become intentionally lost and would spend the better part of an afternoon simply finding my way back. Occasionally I outdid myself and returned home just before dark exhausted, my legs aching, but satisfied that I had, in the course of the day, happened on yet another beautiful, lonely spot which I would never be able to find again. It gave me a sort of perverse pleasure to know that such undiscovered, and perhaps undiscoverable, places existed.

During the second spring that I lived there, I set out for a walk on a classically beautiful morning in May. The flush of new leaves was just out on the woodland trees so that the whole forest was filled with a dappled splatter of light, reminiscent of a pointillist painting; the air was warm, birds were singing, and I began running when I got into the woods and soon reached the edge of my known world. I crossed a stream, climbed a hill, and raced down the other side into a small ravine with a soggy floor. I climbed out, walked over more hills, crossed another stream, and began to head west, toward an area I knew where there were no trails or roads. I got another burst of energy and, just to put myself farther afield, began running with wild abandon. I imagined that something was chasing me. I could almost hear its steady panting, and I ran all the harder until I dropped, wonderfully exhausted, on the slope of one of the hollows.

Suddenly behind me I heard a bird call that I had never heard before. I was familiar with most of the local bird songs, but this was something entirely out of the ordinary, a low, flutelike whistle, very much like a thrush song but somehow unbirdlike. I got up to follow the sound and saw, standing behind me, leaning casually against an oak tree with one leg propped up behind him, a wild man. He was full-bearded, with a long tangle of hair that fell to his shoulders, and he was dressed in a motley combination of denim and khaki and the skins and fur of animals. He had a deerskin cape thrown across one shoulder, and slung across the other shoulder was a sack or pouch also made from animal skin.

He was one of the craziest-looking people I had seen since I left New York City, but he seemed friendly and relaxed, as if it were perfectly normal for us to meet in the forest at eight o'clock on a May morning. He told me, after a requisite amount of small talk, that his name was not Tarzan or Running Deer, as you might expect, but Bill. It turned out Bill had seen me on many occasions even though I had not seen him. He asked me if I was a marathon runner. "You always seem to be so intent on getting somewhere," he said. I noticed that in spite of his wild appearance, Bill spoke in an educated voice.

It seemed that Bill and I had a lot in common; we were, after all, neighbors in a curious sort of way, and he knew well sections of the woods I thought I was the only one to have discovered. We talked for a while about our neighborhood, and then, with due respect, I thought, I asked him about his costume. He said that he had lived in the woods in various places for almost two years and that he found it more comfortable to dress as the Indians dressed, only he didn't call them Indians. "Our forebears," he said, and then a little later, in another context, "woods dwellers" or "woods-dwelling peoples." He said that several times, I remember, during our first conversation: "woods-dwelling people, such as myself."

It was hard to pin down Bill's age. He had young, clear eyes and a full head of long hair, but his face was creased and weathered and smeared in spots with ash and grime. His hands were rough and scratched, I noticed, and thickly calloused. Bill told me he had been living on the ridge since March, in spite of the late snows. And he told me that before that he had lived here until late December of last year. I was curious to know exactly where, since I had never seen any cabins nearby, and I asked him politely where his house was. He cocked his head in a strange way and a slow, repressed smile crossed his lips.

"Well," he said slowly, nodding his head a little, "I don't exactly live in a *house*. Not a man-made one at any rate."

"You have a teepee?" I asked him.

"No, not that either, not even a wickiup, although two winters ago I lived in one, out by New Boston in the Berkshires."

After a short silence he said abruptly, "I live in a cave now." He seemed a little embarrassed by the fact.

"It's a dry one, I've made it that way. It's not really even a cave. I dug it in one of the hollows. But it's very dry." Quickly he changed the subject and began to talk about bobcats.

"I saw one at dawn one day when I lived in the Berkshires. It was peering into my sleeping quarters. It stayed where it was when I woke up, and it was staring at me with its gray-green eyes. I didn't move for twenty minutes — tried to outstare it, but it finally got the better of me. I had to shift, and when I looked up, it was gone. I thought I had dreamed the event for weeks after — it was so weird — but I saw its scat nearby a few days later. They're common you know, but ordinary people — " and here he tried to correct himself so as not to offend me, "I mean people who don't spend a lot of time in the woods — don't see them."

He went on like this for five minutes or so, telling me about his adventures with bobcats. Then he began to talk about bears, saying that they were common too, and if you frightened one badly, it would walk in a straight line for five days.

I enjoyed his rambling, probably erroneous stories about bears and bobcats, and since I sensed that he didn't want to tell me more about his cave, I didn't ask. I did ask him about his satchel, though, and he willingly turned out the contents. They consisted mostly of roots and tubers; one was a large grayish thing that looked like an overgrown potato.

"This is very rare," he said, "at least in this region. It is a wapato — man of the earth. In all my years here I have only found one. But it is good eating."

He also showed me some arrowhead tubers that he had collected, and a huge fistful of various woodland greens, each of which he described to me. "All this, you see, is my dinner. I don't eat much now that I have stopped hunting. I only hunt in fall and winter. I don't eat much in early spring, but I think that is right. This great spirit that everyone talks about, this thing, whatever it is, provides. Do you understand? Don't get me wrong. I don't believe in a god, not a big one anyway. I believe in the little ones. But I think there is a system of sorts, and it makes sense to eat meat only when there are no plants around. So that is what I do."

Because of the rambling nature of his conversation, his way of crowding everything in on itself and telling me everything all at once, I could have concluded that he was crazy. But I once spent some time alone in the woods myself, and I know what it is like when you see another human being, when you get someone to share your ideas with; I indulged him with silence.

I asked him if he knew whether there were any morels growing in the area; it was the second week in May, the height of morel season. He smiled at me with that almost smug, repressed smile.

"You like morels, don't you?" he said. "I have seen you looking for mushrooms. I like them too. I would tell you where they were, except it wouldn't do you any good."

"Why is that?" I asked.

"Because I have eaten them all up!"

He began to laugh at this, a sort of giggle, and then, as if amused by his own reaction, he giggled louder and then broke into a strange, loonlike laugh. There was something comforting about this, and I began to laugh too.

"Well, I'd better get back," I told him. It seemed an opportune moment to part.

"Oh, well, I'll go back with you," he said.

It crossed my mind that I might have taken on more than I cared to with this man and that he would follow me home and ask to move in, but he seemed to sense my concern.

"I mean I'll go up over the ridge to the hemlock stand you always visit. I don't like to go much beyond there you know."

"Fine," I said. "Why don't you like to go past the hemlocks?"

"You know. Beyond that is the wall, and then down the hill, there . . . well, you know what's there — the road."

He winked at me as if to say that it was beyond physical possibility for him to be near a road. It was obvious, though, that he knew my land. He seemed to know every spot on the ridge.

We were not far from the southern end of the lake, at a low spot where there is a slow-running stream. As we crossed it, he stopped and pulled up some plants that were growing on the bank. There were little pea-sized white tubers along the roots.

"You must know these," he said. "Hog peanuts. They are very good. If only there were more of them."

He washed them off in the water, stripped them from the roots, and ate a few.

"Eat one," he said.

They tasted like raw peas.

As we stood by the stream I noticed that he was younger than I thought. He was not a young-looking older man but a person who had aged early. Life seemed to have weathered him. His face was creased, and his tangled, blondish hair was streaked with gray. I guessed he was somewhere in his thirties.

I saw Bill several times that summer and early fall. He always found me first, announcing himself with bird calls or animal noises and allowing me to discover him.

Our second meeting was on a still, early June afternoon. The only sounds in the forest were the singular buzz of a fly or two and the lazy, repetitive call of the red-eyed vireo. Once again, in the midst of this huge silence, I heard an odd, flutelike whistle, followed by a series of quick snorts, like the grunting of a pig.

"How are you?" he asked. "I see you have come again. We will look for more plants today if you like. I have found a good patch of goldthread. Have you ever tasted it? It is very good for your health — very bitter, but good for you. I make a drink with

it sometimes. Just add it to a little stream water. You want to
see?"

Bill's pace wore me out. He had a high-stepping gait, and he
seemed to have a predilection for the harder, more obscure
routes. He would burrow through dense tangles of shrubs, race
up the side of the hollows, spring over logs and boulders like a
goat. When we finally stopped on a dark bank among some
hemlock trees, I noticed that he was not out of breath.

"I am like you," he said. "I often run through the woods. You
have the right idea. Keep at it and you will someday be able to
run down rabbits and deer. Did you know that I can catch a
rabbit bare-handed? Turn left every time you chase one. After
a short burst it will always turn one way or the other. If you
always turn left, you will catch half the rabbits you run after. I
could show you someday if you like."

He was off again with his machine-gun-like blasts of information. I spent the afternoon with him, wandering through his
domain while he showed me plants and told me about animals
and the adventures he had had on the ridge and in other woodlands he had inhabited.

I met him again during that summer, and then again in the
fall. There was no regularity to our meetings. Sometimes I would
go out into the woods, often to a place where I had met him
before, and he wouldn't be there. Other times I would see him
in unexpected places; once he was very close to my house in the
hemlock grove. Once or twice I tried to find him to introduce
him to my wife and friends, but he never revealed himself then,
even though I had a suspicion that he was watching us.

Bill changed the nature of the ridge for me. I had once enjoyed
a sense of solitude and freedom there, but his presence, the
possibility of meeting him or having him observe me, somehow
populated the whole woodland. Still, I did enjoy talking with
him. He was always so full of information and good spirits. I
could tell from the occasional biological or botanical terms he
used that he must have had some formal education in the sci-

ences, but for all his talk he revealed very little of himself or his past. One October day that year, during the course of a conversation on the coming winter, I managed to spring a personal question on him. I should have known better.

We were discussing animals and the hardships they have to endure during the winter months. I began to talk about the adaptability of the human species, how humans range from the very hottest places on the earth to the very coldest. He looked at me knowingly.

"Ah, well, a man," he said. "A man can get used to anything." He seemed to be indicating by this something more than simple physical survival. "That's not necessarily true of animals," he said. "Not true of the cats. Capture them, cage them, and they die. You don't see that death. But those lions in the zoos of the world, the mountain lions and the tigers. They are all dead. Dead inside, you understand. If they only knew about suicide it would be bad for the zoos."

I noticed that he seemed slightly upset by his own observation. He fixed my eye when he had finished speaking and was uncharacteristically silent for a few seconds.

"But you," I asked. "Why do you choose to live like this, away from all human company? I mean, I understand. But how did you happen to come to this?"

"Long story," he said. "But the truth of it is that this is the proper way to live. All the rest — all those houses and that central heat and processed food. That is a lie. A human being is meant to live in this way. We are animals. You did know that, I hope? Man is a species, *Homo sapiens*. Two million years we lived as I live. A thousand, at most six thousand, we live as you live. So who is right? And I ask you this: Who is the more human of the two of us. You or me?"

"That depends on your viewpoint," I said.

"Time is viewpoint. Two million years, my friend. Maybe more. Go home to your house life now and think. I will see you here again."

"When?" I asked him. "When will I see you?"

"I will see you when I see you."

I thought I heard his whistle a few days later. But when I looked for him he wasn't around. I called, but even though the woods were bare and it was almost impossible to walk without rustling leaves, I neither saw nor heard him. It snowed not long after that day, a light November dusting that left the woodland floor and the fields covered with a patterned mixture of leaves, grass, and snow. In the morning after the snow I went out the back door and up through the gardens to the woods. I saw by his tracks that he had been there. He had come up from the woods above the house, circled the yard, and stood below a large pine tree. Presumably he had been staring through the windows. I had a sharp image of him standing there, his long rat-tailed hair falling about his shoulders, his motley, animal-skin coat wrapped tightly around his upper body, and the little flakes of new snow catching in his graying beard. It all seemed unimaginably forlorn, and later in the day I went out to find him. I felt that he was suffering terribly.

The snow had melted by then and I couldn't find his tracks, and although I went from haunt to haunt hoping to hear his call, the forest was empty. A huge, momentous silence such as occurs only in the bleakest seasons of the year filled the landscape. I began to feel in myself something of the loneliness of this man.

Another incident took place about this time that may have had some bearing on Bill's apparent disappearance. Higgins and I had been visiting Emil and Minna and were returning along the old carriage road that passed their driveway. Just before the intersection with the main road a group of men stepped out of the forest in front of us and waved us down. They were a rough looking bunch with grim, serious mouths, and they were armed. Some had baseball bats, one had a rifle, and another was packing an ammunition belt and a pistol. I pulled over and asked them what they were doing.

"We got some trouble here," one of them said. The others were looking inside the car and peering around into the surrounding forest.

"What kind of trouble?" I asked.

"You live around here?" he countered.

I told him I lived on the other side of the ridge.

"Yeah, well, we got some trouble here," he repeated in a more friendly tone.

"What is it?" I asked.

"In plain English," he said, "peeping Tom."

About half a mile down the road toward the lake there was a little spur road with a group of houses strung along it. Several of the women in the houses had seen a man looking in the first-floor windows. Needless to say, he would disappear into the woods as soon as he was spotted. The men explained that there had been another incident that evening, and the males of the neighborhood had formed a posse to catch the man.

Although I was reluctant to admit it to myself, my thoughts went immediately to Bill. He was, after all, an odd sort, and he had apparently come one evening and looked into my windows. I could have mentioned him to the men, but the thought of them scouring the forest for him, capturing him, perhaps even shooting at him, was too much, and I kept my mouth shut and wished them luck. It occurred to me then that perhaps the tracks I had seen were those of the peeping Tom, and that Bill had disappeared shortly after our last vaguely intimate conversation.

A few days later I went back to Emil's to ask if they had had any trouble with the peeping Tom. I told them about Bill.

"You mean this poor man sleeps in the forest alone?" Minna wanted to know.

"He claims he prefers it. He won't even go near the road."

"We should set out honey for him, maybe?" She laughed.

"He is the Green Man," Emil said. "You have to take care of him. He'll take our chickens otherwise."

"He is who?" I asked.

Throughout history, he explained, a man has appeared in the folklore and mythologies of various cultures who, although human in form, lives in the netherworld between the village and the forest. He assumes various names: Gilgamesh, Osiris, Dionysus, or in Celtic myth Amaethon, the god of vegetation. The legend persisted even after the advent of Christianity in Europe. Medieval peasants were careful to set out gifts of food and drink for the Green Man each night, even though they might themselves be hard-pressed for food. In return, the forest-dwelling Green Man would take care of their crops, their animals, and, if necessary, their children. Sometimes, while gathering nuts or greens in the forest, children would see him, a wild, shaggy figure clothed entirely in green leaves or bark. He was a lonely, isolated character, more comfortable with animals than people, and yet never really free from his civilized roots. Green Men do not live in the wilderness; they prefer the wood lot, the forested wild edges just beyond the grazed meadow.

"This is a harmless man," Minna said. "Who are these ruffians with guns? They watch all night television and think the killer is everywhere."

Minna used to blame almost every human ill on either television, automobiles, or the state.

"So what if he looks in a few windows at night. He's lonely. He needs a woman," she said.

I did not hear Bill's bird notes again that winter, and I would not find his tracks, even after the snows. The following spring I began actively to search for him. Once I thought I heard his low, sweet whistle, but it was only the song of the wood thrush. Again and again that spring, even after I gave up my search, I would be reminded of him by the bird calls, by the sight of the goldthread, the groundnut vine, or the little hog peanuts that grew along the stream by the lake. He seemed to be everywhere on the ridge — in the tree trunks, in the ground cover, the squirrel middens, and the long, lazy call of the red-eyed vireo. I couldn't get him out of my mind.

His almost palpable absence seemed as strong as his presence, and after a year or so, with the onset of the next winter, I began to wonder whether I hadn't simply imagined him. He was, perhaps, not so much an entity as a possibility.

I once asked a psychologist friend of mine what she would say about a man who graduated from Harvard College but spurned his degree and subsisted by taking odd jobs around his hometown. Who never married but loved children and was forever taking them out on forays in the woods and fields. Who lived all his life at home with his parents and sisters. Who, for two years, lived alone in a one-room cabin by a pond in the woods in a section of town where drunks and lowlifes of one sort or another often took refuge. And finally, what would she say if this man announced, confessed, boasted, even, that he was happy living in this manner, that he was right and the world was wrong?

"I would have to say," she answered, "that this poor guy has a serious character disorder. I'm not surprised he says he's happy. These types are often so out of touch. They're really only a step away from psychotic."

"Well, what if this man said that sometimes he felt that he actually ceased to be? That he felt suspended above earth? That he once described his profession as mystic, transcendentalist, and natural philosopher to boot?"

She began to catch on, and when I told her I was describing Henry Thoreau, she accused me of taking things out of context.

But who was this Mr. Thoreau who never married but loved children; who had older women and poets as his confidants; who lived alone by Walden Pond and seemed to attract to himself the wild animals of the forest; who would stand for hours in a single spot studying nature; who waded chest deep into swamps and waited there all morning observing frogs; who watched fish, counted flower petals, and found tonic in wildness?

John Burroughs, writing a generation after Thoreau's death, said he was an American Indian. Emerson said he was "the bachelor of thought and nature." Some describe him in political terms, the founder of the passive-resistance movement, some in philosophical terms, the only real transcendentalist. Some think of him as an essayist, some as a naturalist, and locally — that is, among the people of Concord — he is thought of as a drunk, an eccentric, and a malingerer. Even now, one hundred and twenty-five years after his death, Thoreau still bothers the good burghers of his hometown.

Since everyone else has an opinion, I offer one more: Henry was a Green Man.

The facts speak for themselves. He lived apart, at the edge of the village. There was a frontier beyond him, a true wilderness, but he stayed behind; there are no Green Men in the wilderness. Henry loved animals. Birds would land on his shoulders. Squirrels, to the amazement of visitors, would feed from his hands. He had a pet wild mouse who would climb up his legs and eat cheese from his fingers. He walked in the forest and fields every day. He lived off wild food; he was forever out berrying or fishing. He swam regularly, he talked to woodchucks, and he was more at home in the field and forest that at the dinner table or in the drawing room.

Green Men appear to have existed in every age. It was fashionable on the estates of eighteenth-century England to have one's own hermit in residence in some remote section of the grounds. Charles VI of France, in the spirit of the Green Man, was fond of dressing in green leaves and romping with his friends through the streets of Paris. King Arthur's knights, when they were sick at heart, would retire to the forest and dress in green ivy.

Even in our time Green Men can be found. There is, not far from Walden Pond, a man who lives in the local woods and community gardens and feeds on wild plants and spoiled food from the supermarkets. There was a half-blind man who lived in a makeshift plastic tent in one of Boston's parks for a while. He was a bird man who could identify species by call and knew more about nature than most of the city's sighted residents. And then, of course, there was Bill.

But what makes them go? What was it that drove Bill to the woods? What was it that drove — or, perhaps, more accurately, called — Henry to the woods around Walden Pond?

My eldest brother — known to my children as Uncle Jim — came up for Christmas in mid-December, bringing my eighty-year-old mother along with him. Uncle Jim ensconced himself in the loft of my cottage while my mother stayed nearby at a bed-and-breakfast. Whereas my father, my brother Hugh, and I have kept journals, Jim has always kept a sketchbook. He began drawing as soon as he was old enough to hold a crayon and now supports himself by painting. Unfortunately he is not a good businessman, and the world of galleries and art dealers has kept him frustrated for most of his adult life. But he has nonetheless managed to acquire, through periodic windfalls and the occasional profitable one-man show, enough cash to amass a sizable collection of material goods, mostly from the 1930s.

Uncle Jim is a man stuck in time. It is his studied opinion that the world went into sharp decline after 1938 and has yet to recover. In order to counteract this sad state of affairs he lives as best he can in the brighter world of his imagination. He owns two or three — the number varies periodically — pre-1940 automobiles (machines, he calls them). He has a veritable boat yard of older skiffs, pulling boats, punts, powerboats, sailboats, and work boats; he reads *National Geographic* and *Life* magazines from the 1930s and 1940s, has shelves full of old hardcover books. He makes regular rounds of yard sales, barn sales, secondhand stores, and antique shops, and never, in all his life, has he ever intentionally thrown anything away. At night he dreams of England — green pastures and willow-lined rivers. By day he earns his living by painting the past: sailing ships, romantic harbors, flowery gardens by the sea, summer porches of another era. There is no hope in him. He is a lost romantic.

Uncle Jim arrived on a grim December day, carrying his battered leather-belted suitcase. He is never comfortable doing nothing — he is forever puttering — and, anticipating his arrival, I had arranged a number of projects for him.

For months I had been worried that my children might fall out of the loft some night in their sleep. So, with the help of my daughter, Lelia, Jim and I started to build a rail across the open end of the loft. We bought the wood at the sawmill where I got the lumber for the house. We cut two posts, nailed them between the floor of the loft and the ceiling, and then ran rails from either side of the posts to the sloping walls, thereby enclosing the loft. I noticed that this slight internal improvement seemed to stiffen and strengthen the cottage considerably.

That done, we began building a lean-to shed off the back of the cottage on the north side. We put up a frame, ran a stringer across the back wall of the house, planked the roof, and laid on a roll of roofing paper, intending to shingle later when the weather improved. The lean-to served as a combination woodshed, toolshed, outhouse, and catchall.

After that we took on a few lesser projects. We built a Gothic bird feeder modeled on my cottage. Uncle Jim and my son, Clayton, built a small table; Jim made a few drawings for new outbuildings he thought I should construct in the spring. He taught my daughter about mixing colors; he lectured my mother on her erratic driving; he attempted to persuade my erstwhile wife to use an antique car in her new career as a real estate agent; he searched through the toy stores of Concord for the little model antique cars that he likes to collect; and throughout it all, he ate. He is always eating. He will feed eight to ten times a day, every two or three hours — coffee, doughnuts, bananas, eggs, more coffee; a little later some toast, more bananas (he always carries a bunch in his car); then lunch; then, around two or three, another lunch of bananas; high tea around five; then dinner; drinks with bananas after dinner; and finally, if it is offered, a dessert. In spite of his voracious appetite he is not fat. His constant projects seem to burn off the calories.

On Christmas Day, in the tradition of all good bachelor uncles, he finally relaxed. He had his usual breakfast or two, opened a few presents in the living room, and then set to playing with the children's toys. Since my father's death he has been very solic-itous of my mother. He drives her whenever she takes a long trip, makes sure she has enough to eat and drink, and, unlike either of her other two children, he argues with her. They bicker over details; he worries about her; she worries about him; and in this manner, each worrying over the welfare of the other, they get through life. After they left that Christmas, as after nearly every visit, each called to report on the eccentricities of the other.

"I'm worried about that boy," my mother announced (he is over fifty years old).

"We've got to do something about Ma," my brother said (she has been taking care of herself and her family for sixty years).

With the departure of my mother and Uncle Jim and the onset of the new year, I settled in for the long siege of winter. By now I had my cottage fairly well set to survive whatever January and February chose to throw at New England. I had the place in-sulated; I had enough firewood; I had a good working stove; and the interior of my cottage was snug and warmly furnished. Just to the left of the front door stood an old desk where I kept the journals I was reading. On the right I had a bureau with a fine antique oil lamp. Under the bookshelves on the western wall was the bed that used to belong to my brother Hugh. When he was a child, to the horror of my parents, he had carved his initials in one of the posts, and I could still see them there, darkened and old, like a symbol carved by an Indian.

Beyond the bed was another large bureau where I kept sheets and blankets, and beyond that, in the northwestern corner, a waist-high shelf held a camp stove, my copper water urn, plates, cups, tea, coffee, and a little vodka and sake for chilly evenings when the fire was low. On the east wall were more bookshelves; in the northeast corner I had built a closet with shelves at the bottom where I kept my clothes and hung winter coats and the like, and beyond the closet were more bookshelves. There was a table beside the east wall, an old stuffed chair, and my wood stove. On the back wall of the house stood the antique parlor organ. It was the first thing you would see on entering, and the last thing you would see as you shut the door upon leaving. It had a wonderful Gothic look to it and matched very nicely the exterior of the house. Sometimes, while the fire was catching, I would simply stare at it; I loved the low gleam of the polished wood in the light of the oil lamps, the dark shadows in the intricate carvings that ran up either side, and the glowing white of the ivory keys.

In the loft above the first floor I had put two beds, one double and the mate to my brother Hugh's single bed. I had constructed more bookshelves on the back wall upstairs, and between the beds I kept another desk, one that I had used as a child. It was always warm in the loft, and whenever my children were not staying with me I would sleep there.

The snows, which had made a tentative beginning that winter in December, started in earnest by January. There was a storm shortly after New Year's Day, another a week later, which created a solid base, and then another three or four days after that. It snowed regularly — no great blizzards or ice storms, simply a normal New England winter, with snowfall after snowfall layering up in the forest and over the fields and meadows.

During the summer and fall I used to leave my car down by the road in a little clearing and walk up to the house. But after a week or so of heavy snow I found that even walking was difficult, and the only way in, by mid-January, was to ski. I dug out a little parking area close to the road and packed a trail up through the woods to the cottage. Then I forged another trail down through the meadow to my former house. The difficulty of simply going home, of getting wood, and, most especially, of hauling water to the cottage increased with each new snow. The track deepened and grew narrower until finally it was a mere animal trail through the fields and forest, a slim, curving line that disappeared into the trees.

Around the cottage the hickory trees cracked in the wind, and little patches of snow caught in the crevices of the bark. In the deeper forest to the west of the house, snows collected on the feathery boughs of the white pines, piled up, and then fell to the forest floor in little plumes. Regularly I would ski through the woods to the hemlock grove. I watched there for animal signs, the tracks of raccoons and squirrels, deer droppings and quills of the porcupine. At night in my cottage I listened for the caterwauling of the great horned owls that had once nested in the hemlocks. The world around my place was transformed to an elemental environment of wood and snow and stone. I was more cut off than ever from the outside world. There were no uninvited visitors anymore, no alfresco dinners in my garden — no garden for that matter — and no meadow, only a long pasture of white snow covering walls and trails and all but the spikes of the tree trunks. The wind shot at the eaves beyond the loft, limbs snapped and fell. Death itself stalked the life beyond the walls. But I was happy.

9 *The Other Side*

 ONE NIGHT early that winter, after the leaves were off the trees, I noticed a bright halo of light in the sky above the hill on the other side of the valley. The glow was from the new Digital plant. I noticed that it was there, even in the depths of the night, every day of the week; in effect the lights never went off; the glow never went away. I was especially conscious of its presence, since I had become acutely aware of the use of energy for light and heat. I blew out my lamps whenever I left the house even for a little while. I banked my fires carefully and used water sparingly.

Sometimes, seeing the glow, I would think of the loyal penitents, the programmers and engineers, laboring through the night at their computer terminals, alone in their cubicles, with the winds circling the walls outside the plant. I was still curious about the people who worked so long and hard at Digital. Even though I would see them in the town and watch them every morning as they labored up the walkway to the main entrance of the building, I still had not met any of them, and I would find myself wondering what they did in their city on the hill. I used to ask friends who worked for the company what was inside the building, but none could tell me exactly. I did learn something of the life of the Digital employee, though. The people who worked at Digital were intensely loyal. Only two of the many

I talked to that winter spoke critically of the company. One had worked at the Digital Equipment Corporation for twenty years, practically since he was a child. He said he was ready to give up work altogether, get a tent, and spend the rest of his life trekking through the wilderness regions of the world, hoping never again to have to see an industrial building. The other said that he had positive proof that Digital was spying on him through his own terminal. The company was monitoring his private life through a specialized remote sensing system, he said. He was now building a case toward a lawsuit.

Other than these two excommunicants, everyone I met loved the place. They came from a variety of backgrounds. A few were novelists who had finally admitted to themselves that they were not going to be able to make a living by writing fiction. One or two were former teachers, one was a former librarian, one had been a greenhouse worker. There was a housewife, a mechanic, and a perpetual "student of life," as he described himself. In short they were a very unengineerlike group of people.

One of the employees who was most enthusiastic about the company was a divorced friend of mine who had grown up in Schenectady, New York, the daughter of an assembly-line worker. She had married young, had had two children, and had come to the area when her former husband got a job with one of the technological firms along Route 128 outside Boston. Her husband developed a fanatical devotion to his work. He began to spend more time at his office than he did at home, often working through the weekend. When he left her for another woman, neither of the children really noticed since they had hardly known him anyway. He was simply a shadowy figure who had sometimes appeared at their house on Sunday mornings.

After the divorce she began to look for work. She had a high school degree; she had worked for a while in a garden center and as a teacher's aide in her children's school, and she had held a variety of summer jobs, none of which gave her any skills. She did have a high degree of native intelligence, however, and was an avid reader, and when she applied for a secretarial job at Digital she got it, even though she barely passed her typing test.

Six months later she was promoted to a higher-paying job. After a year she applied for another job within the company and got that, too. Step by step she moved up until she was put in charge of a small promotional group, with a staff, a high salary, and a semiprivate office.

"My only complaint about this company," she said, "is that the people on the lunchtime volleyball teams are getting younger and younger, and I can't keep up with them anymore."

Whenever you talk to anyone about Digital, reference will be made to a man known as "Kenny" or "Uncle Kenny." Kenny is Kenneth H. Olsen, founder and chief executive officer of the Digital Equipment Corporation. I happen to work in the town where Uncle Kenny lives, and sometimes in autumn and spring I see him out in front of his substantial but unpretentious home, raking leaves in his shirtsleeves or laboring behind a clunky lawn mower. He shops at the local grocery store. Sometimes I see him there as well, a vague look in his eyes, the lower buttons of his shirt undone, humbly pushing a cart down the aisles, checking the price on each package. Uncle Kenny is, in the view of his employees, a humane, ethical man. By his very nature, his concern for his people, his customers, and his product, he keeps his employees loyal. Uncle Kenny does not drink. He does not approve of drinking, will not allow liquor to be served at Digital social functions. Uncle Kenny believes in keeping his workers happy. He gives them turkeys at Thanksgiving, free dental care, free trips for their children to local amusement parks, as well as all the usual fringe benefits. Uncle Kenny is shy and somewhat bumbling. Once at a Digital Christmas party a friend of mine, who had just started working for the company, was cleaning off a table when a large man passed along the table picking up the scraps and eating them. She turned to him and offered him a wheel of cheese to take home, which he refused.

"Take it," she said. "This is Christmas."

Somewhat embarrassed, he carried it off. My friend turned and saw her boss standing in a nearby doorway, doubled over with laughter.

"Don't you know who that is?" he asked. "That's Kenny Olsen."

Not long after, Kenny himself reappeared in the room, sought out my friend, shook her hand, and told her that the cheese was the best Christmas present he could possibly have received.

Kenny cares. "Do it right," he tells his workers, even if it means disobeying your immediate boss. "Do it right." He rakes his own leaves, is kind to his workers, bestows gifts, is deeply religious. He is also a consummate businessman, ruthless if necessary, dogged, smart, and a skilled manager of people and machines.

Uncle Kenny made his billions by designing minicomputers specifically for engineers and scientists. Before Kenny came along, all computers were immense workhorses stabled in specialized centers and curried only by a few experts. Kenny's small, relatively inexpensive machines gave the computer to the people. Starting with a mere $70,000, in a section of a crumbling woolen mill in Maynard, Massachusetts, he expanded his small company over a twenty-year period into a multibillion-dollar operation. He did this through a combination of striking the right markets at the right time, using unorthodox management techniques, and displaying a willingness to change course whenever it was necessary — not after it was too late. In the parlance of the business community, he never succumbed to what is known as "founder's disease." He learned early on to delegate responsibility, and he decentralized his company. But Uncle Kenny not only transformed the computer industry with his innovations; he also has had a hand in transforming the landscape of eastern Massachusetts. Digital and its many imitators and competitors have been steadily developing some of the last open space in the former farmland and forest just beyond the suburbs of Boston, especially along the major highways.

*

One wouldn't want to take the analogy too far, but there are certain similarities between Kenny Olsen and Henry Thoreau. Both involved themselves with the primary calculation and communication instrument of their age — Uncle Kenny with the computer, Henry Thoreau with the pencil. For all his poetry and mysticism, Henry had an exacting, scientific mind. For years, later in his life, he made his living as a surveyor, and his measurements were so precise they are still used today in Concord. During the mid-nineteenth century the Thoreau pencil became one of the best-known pencils in the United States, thanks in part to Henry's inventiveness.

Henry's father, who ran the family business, was never a rich man. He made do with a variety of small enterprises before he ended up making pencils in Concord in the 1830s. Henry's Uncle Charles had discovered a good source of plumbago, used in making pencil leads, and because of this discovery, and in spite of a certain amount of incompetence in business affairs, the company began to expand. Periodically Henry would work in the family business, and every time he did, he would make some innovation that would improve production. American pencils at the time were inferior to those imported from Europe, especially the German models. American pencil lead was fabricated with plumbago, wax, and glue, and made an irregular, scratchy line. In 1838 Henry did some research and discovered that German pencils were manufactured with Bavarian clay, which was already being imported into Massachusetts. He changed the formulation of the lead and then designed a new grinding mill to produce a fine graphite. The result was a vastly improved American pencil, and the Thoreau family business prospered.

During the winter of 1843–44 Henry once again became involved with the pencil business. He experimented with a new system of baking the graphite and German clay; he invented a machine to cut the graphite, and he designed the pencil so that the wood could be drilled out and the cut lead rammed through the drilled hole. He also developed different grades of lead —

hard line for drafting scientific and engineering work, soft line for art. He became obsessed with pencils and pencil-making machinery that winter. At night he dreamed of new pencil machines. But his obsession was comprehensible; he may have been trying to forget the events that had taken place in winter two years earlier.

On January 1, 1841, Henry's brother, John, was stropping his razor when the blade slipped and cut a nick in the ring finger of his left hand. The wound bled a little, but John bound it up and thought nothing more about it. Later in the week he felt pain in the finger and removed the bandage to look at the cut. It did not seem to be healing properly, so John went to the doctor, who dressed the finger and sent him home. On the way back to the house John felt a sharp pain, not just in his wounded finger but over his whole body. He had to stop on the way, and in fact barely made it home. He went to bed and woke up the next day with a tightness in his jaw muscles. Later that night he was seized with convulsions. Pain shot through his body, and his muscles tightened. The Thoreaus called a doctor from Boston, who arrived in due course, examined John, and announced — one presumes with grave intonation — that nothing could be done: John had lockjaw and would soon die a painful death.

"Is there no hope?" John asked.

"None," the doctor replied.

John was resigned. "The cup that my Father gives me," he said, "shall I not drink it?"

Henry was not so resigned. The Thoreau family was closely knit. Of the four Thoreau children none ever really left home, and none ever married, and the prospect of losing one of the family sent the household into shock. But it was Henry who rose to the occasion.

In early January that year, shortly after John cut his finger, the wind had shifted around to the south, the weather warmed, and the world began to thaw. Under the south winds the snows melted back from the meadows, bees flew from their hives, and little flights of mayflies hovered over the open patches of ground in the forest. Soldier beetles appeared on the south-facing trunks of trees, and plants were putting out leaves. Life seemed to be returning; the world was turned upside down, the seasons reversed. Henry was invigorated. "I derive real strength from the scent of the gale wafted over the naked ground," he wrote. He was uplifted; the earth was his mother, he wrote.

But indoors, sequestered now in his bedroom, the shades drawn against the light, John was dying. His mother and sisters helped John in those last days, but it was Henry who served as the main caretaker. He became an untiring nurse, sitting at John's bedside, talking to him and reading, shepherding him through his frequent periods of delirium. Henry was at his bedside when finally, at two o'clock on a Tuesday afternoon, ten days after he had cut his finger, John died.

In the hours before his death the two brothers talked together quietly in the darkened room. Light commonly sends victims of lockjaw into convulsions, so the curtains would have been drawn against the pale winter sun. They spoke softly together of death and the other side, and then, in the hour before he died, a slow, broad smile spread across John's face. Even in his anguish, Henry could not help but return the smile, and in this manner the two parted company, smiling face to face.

What, one wonders, was there to smile about in so dark an hour? Was the smile caused by the spreading stiffness of lockjaw pulling back the lips in a final death grimace? Or was it knowledge of something on the other shore, something seen by the two brothers in the high, windy spaces of the White Mountains at the culmination of their Concord and Merrimack river trip — some radiance discovered?

Whatever they saw, whatever the two brothers shared in that last hour, it was no consolation. The family mourned openly, but Henry went about the house with a marked serenity and passivity that the family may at first have taken for strength.

Then the calmness deepened into near catatonia. Henry sat un-moving, staring at nothing, saying nothing, barely eating. His sisters led him outdoors, trying to bring him out of this state, but ten days later he too appeared to be dying.

As in life, he followed the path of his brother. Henry's jaws stiffened, the muscles tightened, and lockjaw — or at least all the symptoms of lockjaw — set in. The family called the doctor again. He could find no cut, no cause; but it was clear that Henry was gravely ill, and once again they began to wait for death. Two days later Henry recovered slightly; but then that night the fam-ily brought him more dark news. Henry was fond of children, would spend hours entertaining them with projects, games, and stories. On the night of the twenty-fourth of January one of his favorites, little Waldo Emerson, the child of Henry's good friends Lidian and Ralph, came down with scarlet fever. Three days after Henry received word of his illness the boy was dead.

It was the darkest of winters. Henry stayed indoors in his room. His journals dried up; his excursions into nature ceased; his singing could not be heard; he no longer danced in his sin-gular style. Day after day that winter he remained secluded, depressed, and silent. Then slowly, toward the end of February, signs of recovery began to appear. He reopened his journal. "I am like a feather floating in the atmosphere; on every side is depth unfathomable," he wrote. By March he was writing reg-ularly again. "I live in the perpetual verdure of the globe. I die in the annual decay of nature." And then on March 13: "The sad memory of departed friends is soon encrusted over with sublime and pleasing thoughts, as their monuments are over-grown with moss. Nature doth kindly heal every wound."

The metaphor of natural cycles entered into his writings. He saw renewal all around him, death accompanied by rebirth, and by spring the great unifying theme of *Walden*, the eternal cycle of the seasons, had begun to emerge. It was as if he himself had died with his brother and been reborn. The next six months were a productive period for Henry. For the first time — according to critics, at least — he wrote with a style that was uniquely his own, addressing themes that would concern him for the rest of his life.

Nevertheless, he would die a little every winter. He was depressed and sick again the winter after his brother's death, and it is little wonder that in the following winter — the winter of 1843–44 — he would throw himself into his family's pencil business. Obsession grants forgetfulness. In some ways the rest of his life was a quest for forgetfulness — either that or a memorial.

There was a snowstorm in New England on the one hundred and forty-fifth anniversary of John Thoreau's death, a soft, long fall that piled up on the pine boughs and made fantastic shapes on the rock walls in the woods behind my cottage. The next few days were bitter cold and windy, with hard little plumes of sheared snow curling off the walls and streaming down across the open fields. Late in the afternoon, after the wind dropped, I went for a long ski on the solidly frozen Beaver Brook. I crossed the road, climbed over an old barbed wire fence, and skied down through a sloping old hay field where, some years ago, a small herd of heifers used to graze. The field had grown up in recent years, with multiflora rose, dogwoods, and other open-ground species. Their thorny, brittle stems pierced the snow and stretched their shadows in the late-afternoon light. Beneath the snow and the ice on the brook, somewhere unseen, life continued: fish swam and fed, green plants still wafted in the slow currents, and a few slow-moving, cold-dulled aquatic insects moved here and there. But above, in the open air, the world seemed dead.

I skied for a mile or so down the brook and then began to climb through a series of sloping fields on the other side of the valley. Here, too, the fields had been abandoned. There was an orchard on the north slope, and a small woods of young pines and oaks was taking over another pasture that had once belonged to a farm located in the valley beyond the hill.

By now the sun had set and the sky was darkening, but there was still enough light to reveal the landscape that stretched to the east. This was a Saturday evening; the traffic on Route 495 was light, and the world around me was strangely silent. Behind me, to the west, in the red sky I could see the ridge where my little cottage was situated. Below were the hay fields of the abandoned farms, the wide flood plain of Beaver Brook, and the fields and orchards of the farm I had just crossed.

This particular farm offered one of the more pleasing landscapes in the region. I used to walk there often, but for some reason I could never warm to the place, in spite of its beauty. There was something strangely lonely and ominous about the land, some vague cloud that hung over it. I couldn't understand why I was so uncomfortable there, but then a few years ago I received a letter from a woman who had grown up on the farm. She told me that long after her family had left the place, after the house and barn had been torn down by the land developer who purchased the property, she used to come back and tend the little flower beds that she and her mother had worked while she was growing up. "After they discovered the body," she wrote, "I haven't been able to go back. Something changed." It seems that the corpse of a murder victim had been found in the foundation of the house.

The wind came up once the sun dropped, a chill, bitter spear that shot across the lower fields and skidded up the slopes. I turned my back to it and faced the southeast. Beyond me I could see the light of the old town center, bright and twinkling in the frigid air, but the better part of the view was cut off by the great square Digital building with its cold glare of lights. There were, I presumed, very few people working that Saturday night — a few devoted programmers perhaps, or maybe a cleaning crew — and yet the entire building was illuminated. Unlike the twinkling glimmer of the town, this light gave no warmth. It lit the dark landscape with a hard gleam that reflected off the snow, turning it a lurid green.

"Nothing," Henry Thoreau wrote, "is so opposed to poetry — as business."

Weather such as we were having made me worry about Sanferd Benson in his old house in Concord, and Prince Rudolph at the Route 495 cloverleaf. Benson, I presumed, was faring well enough, since he at least had a roof over his head. Prince Rudolph was more of a concern. It was hard for me to believe that an older man, especially one with a taste for alcohol, could survive some of the windy, zero-degree nights we were having, sleeping by a campfire in his overcoat, covered by cardboard boxes and blankets. But periodically I would see Rudolph in town, marching determinedly from his campsite to the local grocery store or back again.

By this time Rudolph would condescend to greet me when we met, and perhaps share a few words, although he was still aloof, as if I were a member of some lower caste of humanity and he was the King of the Road — which in a sense he was. He was one of the most independent people I had ever run across.

I saw him that month on one of those brilliant January days when the sun off the snow is so bright it hurts your eyes.

"Get through last night okay?" I asked him as I overtook him.

"Wouldn't be here if I hadn't, would I?"

"Guess not," I said and began to move on.

"Well, you guessed right. You're a smart kid, aren't you."

I picked up my pace a little; it was clear he was not in a friendly mood. I heard something snort behind me and saw that he had tripped and gone down on his knees in a snowbank. Without thinking, I went back and helped him up by the arm. He smelled of drink.

"Get your hands off me, Jack, I can handle this," he said. Then almost immediately he changed his stance.

"Oh, hey, I'm sorry," he said. "Accept my apology, all right?"

"Sure. It's a cold day."

"No, I mean it. I want you to accept my apology."

"Right," I said. "I accept."

"No, I want to apologize."

"It's all right, really."

"Bad day here. I got a kid, you know. He lives in Leominster. Son of a bitch kicked me out. He remarries, and she says 'no room,' but I want to apologize to you."

"I understand," I said. "You're doing all right."

"You bet, Jack. Cops come by again last night. I told them to get lost. Who needs that stuff."

"You're doing all right as you are."

"You bet. I raised that kid, know what I mean? You know what it is to raise a kid? And anyway, it isn't him. It's her. The bitch. French-Canadian."

"Maybe you should go back?"

"I do go back. Sometimes I go there when she ain't around. He says it's okay, come back. I say . . . You know what I say to them?"

"What?"

"No, seriously, you know what I say?"

"What?"

"I say I'm happy like I am. I don't want to live in no house anymore. Too hot. All that talk. Sometimes it used to be too much. Yap, yap, yap. I say 'shut up or I'm leaving,' and they say 'so leave.' The sons of bitches. I'm sixty-two years old."

"You're better off this way."

"Damn right."

"I just wonder how you get through these zero-degree nights. I'm cold where I live, and I've got a stove."

"Let me tell you something, kid. You get used to it."

Mr. Benson, who eschewed alcohol his entire life, who would work steadily from the time he got up in the morning until he went to bed at night, with perhaps a short break for an afternoon nap, was in far better shape than Prince Rudolph, even at ninety-four. I went down his road on a warm day that month to look for him and found him in an alcove of his house, steadily chopping an old crate into kindling wood. We went through the business of reintroduction, and then, after it became clear that he did indeed remember me, I asked him how he was doing.

"Not too well this year, I'm afraid. I've been in the hospital."

He tapped his chest, and to spare him a recitation of the gory details, I changed the subject. He seemed cheery enough and quite alert that day, so I asked him if he knew my friends Higgins and Jane.

"Jane? Well, I don't know, maybe, I meet so many people."

As far as I knew, except for his nephew, myself, Higgins, Jane, and the mailman, no one else ever came down his driveway.

"Jane is interested in your stories about the river here," I said.

"Yes, well, it was very interesting here. There used to be more river traffic than there is today. There was once a fire, you know, down at the boathouse."

I knew about that fire. The blaze had occurred in about 1922 and had destroyed all the rented canoes, rowboats, and steam-powered launches that used to come up the river past Benson's place. He would tell me about it almost every time we met.

"That's the kind of thing we want to hear about," I said.

"Well, I can tell you about that."

"We want to get your story on film." I was certain he had never heard of a video camera.

"Well, I don't know about film."

"It's nothing really."

"Well, I don't have much to say."

"That's all right. We just want to hear about your life here and the old days."

"Well, I can tell you about that I suppose. But one year is just like another, don't you know. You plant, and you weed, and you harvest. There was a flood one year, 1938 I believe."

"That's good."

"It was a hurricane."

This too was a story I had heard before. The sun was beginning to set and it was getting colder, so I extricated myself and promised to come back in a week or so to introduce him to Jane. He seemed in fine health that day. I didn't know his clock was running down.

I used to know an old man who lived on one of the farms to the west of the ridge on which my cottage was located. He said he loved to sit at his window at night and look east to the black line of the ridge in winter. "The trees there were so dark," he told me. "They made you think that something could happen in there."

Henry Potter was a wealth of information on that part of the world. His great-grandfather had moved to the place early in the nineteenth century, and he had another relative, a carpenter, who had kept a diary of his daily life for a few years. Potter used to tell me about Indians. He claimed his great-grandfather had had trouble with marauding crop thieves.

"Mind you," Potter said, "Indians were wiped out a hundred years before, but the old man still believed they were there. They used to hide out on the ridge, he said. 'Course I don't believe that. But if there were Indians around here still, given present conditions, that's where they would go."

This was about four years after I had last seen Bill, the Green Man, and I risked telling Potter about my adventures with this modern-day version of a hunter-gatherer.

"Well, it don't surprise me none. Earlier times you had strange types living back there in the hollows. Old Man Jensen used to see people all the time."

Jensen was a farmer who, in the early 1920s, had gone crazy, burned down the local one-room schoolhouse, and then shot himself behind one of his barns.

"That's what sent him over the line, you know. He saw Indians in the woods back there. He thought they were out to get him."

I was thinking of this conversation during that month. Higgins and I had taken a walk on the ridge in the middle of a snowstorm and had gotten lost. There had been a few flurries starting up when we left, but after half an hour or so, when we were deep inside the forest, the flurries had increased to a driving snow which started to obliterate our tracks. We turned around to go back as soon as we realized the intensity of the storm, but for some reason failed to find familiar landmarks — a large boulder shaped like a whale, the old oak tree on the carriage road, and similar navigation points. We were still able to pick up our trail, though, and we kept going, sure that in time we would pass something we recognized. After about another half-hour or so, we came to the realization that we were going around in circles.

"What do you think?" I said.

"Let's go around again and watch for the spot where we started into the circle. There's got to be a straight line somewhere."

"Provided the snow hasn't covered it yet," I said.

We started walking fast so as to find the spot before the snow covered it entirely. I felt a little foolish getting lost in my own backyard, but then I was forever getting lost there. We came to a likely-looking place in the circle — not a clean track of footprints by any means, but simply a narrow groove winding off through the forest. It seemed to me to be heading in the wrong direction, though.

"You're lost," Higgins said. "This has got to be it. Nothing else out here makes tracks that deep."

I turned around to see how fast the track we had just made was filling up and, about twenty yards back, saw a man standing by one of the oaks, his hand resting on the side of the trunk. He didn't move when I spotted him; he stood there watching us. I thought it was Bill, come back. He was wrapped in some kind of brown robe that, from where I was standing, looked to be made from fur or skin, and he had on one of those round fur hats that trappers in the American West used to wear.

"Higgins, look at this," I said.

He turned around and stared back along the trail.

"Look at this guy back here. He's been following us."

Higgins looked, shaking his head.

"Where?"

I raised my arm to point. There was a gust of wind. The trees shuddered and dropped a branchload of snow somewhere nearby. I turned to look, and when I turned back, the figure was gone.

"You're losing it," Higgins said.

"Maybe so."

I wanted to go over and look for tracks, but Higgins insisted we follow what we presumed to be our trail before it too filled with snow and left us stranded there for the night. I followed him, and in time we got to the hemlock grove and were able to follow the stone walls out to my cottage. We made tea and took a snort of Stolichnaya.

"Maybe it's all true, Higgins. Maybe there are bears and Indians and ghosts and murderers living back there in the hollows."

"Maybe you need a break," he said.

10 Life on Earth

 AS THE WINTER DEEPENED, living in the cottage became increasingly difficult. If I spent a night or two away, as I sometimes did, I would return to find the house stone cold, the water frozen in the urn. I would have to spend an hour or so shivering by the stove while I built up the fire. Even when I hadn't been away, the chill mornings made me stiff and achey until I could get the fire churned up and brew some hot coffee. I was also tired of brushing snow off my various woodpiles, and then having to clean up the mess I made hauling in the wood.

I had come to appreciate my small life in spite of these inconveniences. It was essential living, as Henry used to say. I found that sitting outside, even in cold weather, was not uncomfortable. The trees sheltered me from the winter wind, and whenever it was sunny, which it often is in New England in January, I could make tea on my terrace and relax in a chair, reading in the sun, feeling a little like a nineteenth-century tuberculosis patient. Nevertheless, during February that year I took Higgins' advice and left the cabin for a week.

I had long been interested in the radio telescope at Arecibo, Puerto Rico, in the hills not far inland from the northern coast. A friend who used to work there told me stories of the beautiful landscape in the region and of the curious ideas people there had about the telescope. The radio telescope was surrounded by small subsistence farms, and many of the farmers were suspicious of the strange device. Some were convinced, she told me, that the telescope was communicating with the spirit world or was being used for black magic. Others believed that it was a landing place for aliens. Strange entities had been seen in the hills, according to a few of the local farmers. Devil children had been born to some of the women. Cows had died mysteriously; goats behaved in an odd manner; and one night a thing with red eyes appeared in a barn among the goats, carrying a headless chicken. The people had heard unearthly barks and howls emanating from the valley where the telescope was located.

I thought this had the makings of an interesting article, and that winter I got an assignment from a magazine to go to Puerto Rico to do the story. I flew down on a Sunday in the middle of February, just in time to escape a terrible ice storm that swept through New England. I rented a car in San Juan and drove inland to spend the night on a coffee plantation in the center of the island. The next day I drove to the hills around the radio telescope, stopping often at local cantinas to eat and talk to people. I was in no hurry to get to the observatory, since part of my story — the major part in fact — was about the local reaction to the telescope.

I had a few contacts on the island, one of whom was an older North American woman who lived alone on a mountain top on a small coffee plantation. She turned out to be a spirited old leftist, politically active in both Puerto Rico and the States. She and her husband had bought the plantation some twenty years earlier as a vacation spot, and after her husband retired the two of them began to live there year-round. He died shortly after they settled in Puerto Rico, but she carried on by herself, alone on her mountain top, surrounded by small vegetable plots, old coffee trees, and tropical birds. She had a wonderful view of the surrounding mountains from her place — wild, rounded hills, a flowing tropical sky, and dark, shadowy valleys. As we ate lunch on the terrace, she told me that what my friend had said about the telescope might not have been quite accurate.

"The issue with the observatory, if there is an issue, is that people around here think it might have something to do with the military," she said. "That's the real story. I can give you names. But I'm not sure you'll find any truth in all this. People around here are quite afraid of American military installations. Properly so, of course, but I don't think Arecibo has anything to do with 'Star Wars,' and I don't think you'll find anyone who believes the place is involved with black magic."

The next day I drove inland toward the observatory from the city of Arecibo, along ten or twelve miles of narrow, winding roads that cut through the bizarre karst country of the north coast. Because of the natural erosion of the limestone outcroppings, the countryside has been reduced to a series of sharp green hillocks, some with sheer limestone cliffs overhung with luxuriant tropical vines. As the narrow road snaked inland away from the brighter, more developed coast, it passed through small green villages with open-air bars or grocerias, where the men of the village would be standing around talking. I would stop and talk with them. They were friendly and happy to chat, but I could not find anyone who believed that there were spirits emanating from the crater in which the radio telescope was located. Most of them, I decided, were too young and cynical to believe in spirits anyway. Some had been to New York City and had relatives there.

I drove on, dodging the cows and chickens wandering in the road, stopping often to ask more questions. The air was filled with the rich sounds of tropic life, distant drumming, bird song, the lowing of cows, and everywhere the whistlelike call of the *coqui,* a small tree frog that is an integral part of the folk life of the island. At one place I came to a crumbling chapel just off one of the back roads, and as I walked around, an old priest came out and blessed me.

"What do you know of this observatory, Father?" I asked. "Is it a good thing?"

"Good perhaps, and bad perhaps." He tipped his hand from side to side with a shrug. "People talk about it. Visitors come from the coast to see it. But look at my church. What can we do?" There were fissures in the stucco walls of the chapel and grass growing in the cracks of the cement courtyard in front of the entrance. In back a broken window overlooked a small, untended garden.

I had heard that there was a small village very near the observatory where a group of families lived without running water or electricity, in the very shadow of one of the most sophisticated electronic devices in the world. I tried to find the place but became hopelessly lost. At one point the road I was on seemed to give out altogether. I turned back, and on the way out saw an old man with a narrow, hatchetlike face standing barefoot in a shallow swale, his pants rolled up. He held a homemade vine rope in his left hand, and at the other end of the rope was a handsomely patterned heifer. Both were staring at me.

"Do you know how to get to the observatory from here?" I asked, after proper introductions.

"No," he said.

"You have heard of it?"

"Yes. Much."

"Maybe I should continue back this way?" I asked.

"Maybe."

"You have been there?"

"Not me."

He was about seventy or eighty years old, but with the healthy nut-brown skin and bright black eyes of a younger man. I changed the subject and asked him about his cow, and he became more talkative.

"She is a good heifer," he said. "Tinta is her name." He yanked her over to him and scratched her neck.

I introduced myself and explained my mission, and he told

me his name was Ramón Gonzales and he had been born in this
valley seventy-six years ago. Ramón had a farm near the swale.
When he grew too old for heavy work, he turned the farm over
to one of his sons, who eventually went off to New York. A
younger son took over and Ramón stayed on, daily taking Tinta
to the high meadows to graze.

"I am waiting for entry into heaven," he said with a smile.

I asked him again if he knew anything about the observatory.
"What do they find there, I wonder?"

"Stars and moons," he said authoritatively.

"Planets?"

"Yes, planets. And moons. Stars and other things — things
people cannot see. These they can see."

He shifted his stance and waved his arm in the direction of
the observatory and nodded slowly.

"They see many things there. You should be careful. Don't
ask too many questions when you get there."

He came up out of the swale drawing Tinta after him and
stood closer to me, taking my arm.

"Where are you from?" he asked.

"Boston."

"I have no cousins there," he said. "Why is it that you want to
know about this observatory?"

"I have heard that other things happen there that they don't
talk about. I heard this from a friend, and I'm curious about it."

"You should be careful."

"I know."

"Maria Puente? Do you know her?"

"No."

"She was pregnant and lost the child. Later she went to the
front gate and shouted at them and cried. Guards came out.
Police came and took her away."

"Why did she get angry? What did they do to her?"

"It was not them. It was the machines. You be careful. Just

when you get there, don't ask too many questions. Just be careful."

He pulled Tinta away from some weeds she was eating and for some reason became annoyed with her.

"*Vaya!*" he shouted. "*Vaya, vacita!*" He pushed her toward some other plants and came over and took my arm again.

"I know the purpose of that place," he said. "They tell us here on the island that they are looking for stars, but that is not true."

"What are they looking for?"

He glanced over his shoulder.

"*Buscan la cara de Dios,*" he said intimately. "But I will tell you this. They send out to search for God, but what they attract to the valley are spirits. Bad spirits. They give you tours of this place. The people go there. But there is one section where no person from the islands can ever enter. Dogs are there, as high as Tinta."

He raised his arm to his shoulder. I had heard this story before, in one of the cantinas where I had stopped. But the man who told me was drunk. Ramón was not drunk.

"How do you know this," I asked politely, "if you have never been there?"

"El Negrito told us," he said.

The drunk man at the cantina had mentioned El Negrito too, and in another village someone else had told me that the only spirits he knew about were the ones El Negrito spoke of.

El Negrito was from the coast, I had been told. A slight, intense, black man with green eyes, he had worked for a while as a janitor at the observatory. He had access to certain keys, and at night would range freely around the place, pushing buttons. El Negrito was said to be the apprentice to a *curandero,* a white witch, also from the coast, who had sent him on a mission to find out about the observatory. The *curandero* did not like it that the place seemed to have a magical power, people said.

El Negrito would frequent the local bars and tell people what he saw at Arecibo. There were dogs inside the observatory; chickens were sometimes sacrificed; electrical forces were attracted to the central dish and could bring dead things back to life. Throughout the day and night the scientists would search the skies, trying to attract spirits.

El Negrito himself seemed to have become something of a folk hero, at least in the more remote villages. He told people he could walk on air; he told them his teacher could raise the dead, and he said that he had spoken to Jesus on many occasions. He was a skilled drummer and had played at some of the local Pentecostal churches.

"Some of what El Negrito says is not true," Ramón told me, "but much is fact. This I know. For example, I have heard the dogs howling. And if you ask any person here, he will tell you that there is an area inside the observatory where no outsider has been. None but El Negrito.

"You be careful," Ramón said, as we parted. "They will be nice to you, but don't ask too many questions."

The observatory is surrounded by a high hurricane fence topped with barbed wire, and the entrance is an immense, electronically operated slide gate controlled by a uniformed guard. I spoke to the guard about getting a tour, and he made a phone call and then pushed a button. The gate slid open and I was greeted by my guide, a svelte young Puerto Rican woman who told me she had grown up in Queens, New York. She would be taking me and a group of Colombians through the observatory. Fluent in English and Spanish, she rattled off technical information with machine-gun rapidity, alternating between the two languages.

The actual radio telescope, the largest and most sensitive device of its kind in the world, consists of a 100-foot reflector covering the floor of a crater. Hovering 450 feet above the great dish of the reflector are 40,000 adjustable aluminum panels mounted on a 630-ton suspended framework.

The telescope presents an ironic contrast to the surrounding landscape, with its savage karst hillocks, lush tropic vegetation, and the constant, unending call of the tree frogs. The reflector dish collects natural radio signals emanating from galaxies, erupting stars, clouds of gas, pulsars, and quasars. The radio energy given off by these bodies is detected, amplified, and passed through cables to a control building, where the information is analyzed. The whole system can be reversed so that a transmitter in the carriage house above the dish sends radio energy to the reflector, which then beams the signals to space or to a specific target. Data extracted from the radio emissions from the far-off regions of the universe allow astronomers to measure distances and masses of galaxies and gather information about the stars in our own galaxy.

Periodically the system closes down its normal research operations and searches the sky for signals from extraterrestrial civilizations. So far, no messages have been received.

I had arranged to talk to the public relations director, the man responsible for disabusing the local people of their myths concerning the observatory. The interview was desultory. As we talked, he perched on his desk, picking his teeth, flirting with the tour guide. He didn't know anything about spirits.

"It could be some of the old people back in the little villages believe that sort of thing. Not the school kids though. They know more about space than me. They're into it. And there are no dogs here."

I asked him about the sections of the observatory where no visitors are permitted.

"The computer room," he said. "We keep people out simply because scientists work day and night in there and don't want to stop every ten minutes to explain to the tourists what they do. Anna takes care of that, don't you, Anna?"

"I take care of those tourists," she said.

"Anna takes care of everyone."

"I'll take care of you, big boy, unless you shut up."

He tried to grow serious.

"I go around to the schools. I must do fifty tours a year. Kids come here. There's no controversy."

I asked him about the woman who had miscarried.

"It's true. Once in a while someone loses it, and the old superstitions resurface."

"She was a *loca*," Anna said. "I was here that day. She was screaming and yelling about bad waves. Just another *loca*."

"No story here, I guess, about spirits and cargo cults and conflicts with the locals, that sort of thing?"

"No story. The big story's out there." He glanced toward the sky.

I left Arecibo on a Sunday night and drove to San Juan on back roads that twisted through the hills past small villages, each with a church service taking place. Many of the villagers in that section of the island were Pentecostal, and they had transformed the services into something on the outer edges of the traditional Christian church. In each village I heard maniacal drumming spilling out of the brightly-lit hillside church buildings, echoing through the hot night. Most of the churches kept their doors and windows wide open, and in some I could see crowds of people standing just inside the doors, swaying. Occasionally I could hear singing, a high descant chorus sung in fifths, with atonal melodies and a distinctly African flavor. The songs intertwined with the relentless drumming and the sharp whistles of the *coqui*. At a turn near one of the churches my headlights illuminated a woman standing in the road. Dressed in a long skirt, with gray hair falling about her shoulders, carrying a long staff, she looked like a witch or a madwoman. When she saw the car, she glared, ducked off the road, and hid in the bushes.

I fell asleep on the plane back to Boston and had a short, brilliant dream about Ramón and the witchlike woman on the road. They seemed to be involved in some sort of ritual associated with the chain link fence in front of the Arecibo observatory. I was disoriented when I awoke. It took me a minute to accustom myself to the quiet lights of the plane, the sleeping passengers, the murmur of voices, and the dull roar of the jet engines. Streaking across the night sky toward Boston, suspended thirty thousand feet above the sea, I felt at that moment a great rush of gratitude for the airplane and for the pilot and his crew. This was followed by a strange feeling of affection for technology — quite out of character for me. Technology reminded me of home and the Digital plant and Uncle Kenny and his workers, and suddenly all the opposing forces on the ridge seemed to merge into a grand pattern in which nothing really mattered. The great sweep of geological time would resolve all, and ours seemed such a lovely, dualistic, yet essentially benign period in which to be alive.

I shifted in my seat. I looked out at the black passage of the night, and then I resolved to renew my effort to get inside the Digital plant — not because I wanted to explore and expose some enemy, the despoiler of pear orchards, but because I had become genuinely interested in the way in which the world works.

Henry Thoreau used to leave his cabin at Walden from time to time. He often had dinner with family or friends, and he moved out while he was plastering the walls before his first winter there. He also left one afternoon in July 1846 and did not return for the night. He had gone into town to pick up a shoe and while he was there happened to meet Sam Staples, the local tax collector and jailer. Staples reminded Henry that he had not paid his poll tax in several years and that unless he paid sometime soon, Staples would have to do something about it. Henry announced, with characteristic acidity, that he did not intend ever to pay his poll tax. Staples said that if he didn't pay, he would have to lock him up. There was another little exchange, and then Henry was escorted to the jail house, where he spent the night in a cell with a man accused of burning down a barn. During the night someone in a nearby cell set up a chant. "What is life?" he called out again and again. "So this is life?"

It was a good question, just the type of thing that interested

Henry Thoreau. He listened for a while and then put his head to the bars and shouted back, "Well, what *is* life, then?"

The fellow prisoner ceased his chant; silence returned to the jail. There were no answers as yet.

Henry was released from jail the next day; a woman, probably his Aunt Maria, had undermined his act of civil disobedience by paying Staples the required amount. Reluctantly Henry left jail, picked up his shoe at the cobbler's, and was seen berrying that afternoon with a group of children on a nearby hill. By night he was back at Walden.

Henry left his cabin a little more than a month later for an excursion with a cousin to the Maine woods. Coincidentally, perhaps, he departed on the same day that, seven years earlier, he and his brother had left for their Concord and Merrimack river trip, the account of which he was writing in book form while he was living at the cabin at Walden Pond. His intention on the Maine trip was to climb Mount Katahdin, which, in 1846, had been scaled only four or five times before. He was now twenty-nine. His brother was dead; he was living alone for the first time in his life, and he was embarked on a path as a writer.

Henry left Concord, traveled to Bangor by rail and boat with his cousin, and then continued some sixty miles north to the Indian village of Oldtown, where he met with several of the inhabitants. He pushed on, and on one of the islands in the Penobscot River — most of which were inhabited by Indians — he met a couple of moose hunters who planned to leave the next day for the north, heading in the same general direction as Henry and his cousin. Thoreau persuaded them to help guide him, and the group arranged to meet the next day at a dam site farther north on the West Branch of the Penobscot. They picked up two more for their party at Mattawamkeag and pushed upstream to the house of a local pioneer, a man named Uncle George McCauslin. There, in the rain, they waited, and when the Indian hunters never showed up, they persuaded Uncle

George and another local to accompany them into the unknown country beyond the rivers to the slopes of Katahdin.

They were now about thirty miles southeast of the mountain. There were six in the party; they had a few barrels of pork, fifteen pounds of hard bread, a frying pan, a kettle, blankets, and a strip of cotton cloth to rig as a tent. They loaded everything into a batteau, a large, dorylike vessel, and pushed off. Henry was no novice when it came to boat handling, but he was especially impressed with the work of the two local men. Uncle George stood in the stern, his companion, Tom Fowler, in the bow. Working in concert, with long spruce poles tipped with an iron shoe, they forced their way up the Millinocket River for some two miles over rocks and rapids. The group came to Quakish Lake and rowed another two miles across to the river on the other side.

A forest of spruce and cedar lined the shore, overhung with gray lichen; ducks rose and sailed across the sky, a loon settled and laughed maniacally, and the still atmosphere had, according to Henry, a ghostly prospect. The trees were mere spirits of themselves. Beyond they could see Mount Katahdin, its summit lost in the clouds. To Henry it looked like "a dark isthmus — connecting the heavens with the earth."

They reached the dam at the end of the lake and pushed on to the head of North Twin Lake. Night was approaching, but because the lake was still and the rowing easy, they decided to keep going. The sun went down, the sky turned red, and the moon rose. They began to sing as they rowed, old traditional tunes of the French *voyageurs* who first pushed into this wild country. The moon crossed the sky, and at the head of the lake the island where they intended to camp appeared in the moonlight. They rested on their oars, ceased their singing, and listened for the answering call of wolves, a common sound in that country — and, as Henry says, a dismal and unearthly sound. There was only silence; and then, from somewhere in the forest, a deep-voiced owl called. They watched for moose and bear and caribou, took up their oars and songs again, and early in the night they reached a camping site McCauslin knew about.

There in the dank forest they built a fire, set up their tent, and prepared to sleep. The wind came up; sparks drifted from the fire and the tent caught and burned. Seemingly undismayed, they hauled the boat up on the shore and slept under it. Periodically someone would get up and feed the fire, which, in spite of their earlier disaster, they kept burning all night. Grotesque and fiendlike shadows were thrown up against the surrounding trees. The men lay there, each presuming the others to be asleep but all of them wide awake.

The moon and stars were still shining when they finally got up just before dawn and pushed on across the lake. The day was clear and the water was calm, and the surrounding mountains were reflected in its surface, all dominated by Katahdin, with its flat, high tableland. All that day they rowed over lakes, pushed up the rapids of small, hard-running rivers, came to lakes again, crossed, rested, ate, and rowed, portaging their heavy batteau around waterfalls, and at one point warping it over a set of falls. With great difficulty they forged through stiff rapids, the batteau almost perpendicular to the stream. One of the poles snapped at a critical moment on that stream, but Henry snatched up a spare and passed it back to the sternman just in time to save the crew. Finally they reached the mouth of Murch Brook, about fifteen miles from the summit of Katahdin, and here, on level ground, they made camp and fished until dark, hauling in a good mess of trout and roach.

That night Henry dreamed that he was trout fishing. The dream must have been intense. It woke him up, and in the dark mystery of the new territory he could not be sure what was dream and what was life, so he got up, baited his hooks, and began fishing in the darkness. In the moonlit night, the dark image of Katahdin stood distinctly outlined against the sky. Close at hand the dark stream rippled past; the wilderness stretched around him. He cast; a fish struck; and there, in the black night, he hauled in speckled trout and beautiful, silvery roach. They cut an arc against the black silhouette of the mountain; they flew across the air like mystical flying fish. Henry "found the dream to be real."

The next morning the men made a cache of their supplies, hanging everything from the tops of saplings to save it from the bears, strapped on their packs, and hiked toward the mountain. They were in new territory now. Neither McCauslin nor, in all probability, any other white man had passed through this area, and they navigated mainly by Henry's compass orientation. All day they pushed through the forest and up the slopes of Katahdin itself, until finally, about four o'clock, in view of the summit, they made camp.

They must have been tired by this time; they had not brought much food and were living mainly on fish and berries; they had slept little, and they were traveling through what must have been a difficult and in some places nearly impassable forest. Nevertheless, while the others made camp, Henry continued up the mountain slopes. He followed the course of a stream bed, and at some points had to climb around waterfalls, pulling himself up by roots and tree trunks. Once he had cleared the tree line, he could look back across the countryside below him, a great wild and houseless land. The stream he was following, about thirty feet wide in places, rushed past him in a great washing tide. He came into an odd, broken land strewn with immense boulders. Black spruce trees grew in the crevices between them, so thick and ancient they were able to support his weight. More or less walking on the tops of trees, he climbed upward. Below him in spots he could see into the dark crevices, where he was convinced that bears, "even then at home," were sleeping. At sunset he came to a spot where gray, silent rocks surrounded him like sheep. The skirt of a cloud filtered ahead of him. He stopped. And then he turned around and went back to his companions and the light of the fire. They were awakened that night by a horrific scream. One of the party had dreamed that the world was on fire.

Ever since they had left the rivers and headed into the woods, Henry had taken the lead. The next day once again he led the way, and soon he had left the others behind. He was intent on making the summit. Once more he ascended the great stepped shelves of the mountain slopes, quickly passed the altitude he had attained the previous evening, and walked into the bank of clouds, traveling upward but now surrounded by the swirling mists.

Long before he even began the ascent of Katahdin, he had been thinking of the otherworldliness of the mountain. He had asked Joe Neptune, one of the Indians he had met earlier, if he thought that Pomola, the avenging spirit of Katahdin in the local Indian mythology, would allow them to attain the summit. As he had moved upward the day before, he had imagined Satan in Milton's *Paradise Lost* struggling up out of chaos. Now, almost at his destination, the mystic image sharpened. The clouds thickened and swirled, broke to reveal the sky, and then closed in again, sweeping across the rocky wild scarp. Dank crevices and crags surrounded him. In such a place, he thought, Prometheus was bound while eagles tore at his liver. In such a place Atlas stood. Here an altogether indifferent nature had got human life at a disadvantage. The gentle image of nature, the kind, quiet-flowing waters of the lily-strewn Concord River, the pastoral landscape of fields and woods was banished. Here was the unfinished, wild planet, a place of the gods, not yet tamed for their human children. Entering this realm was an insult to them, he thought, and suddenly, there on the heights, amid the charged mists, they shouted out at Henry Thoreau, "Why came ye here before your time?"

He had not yet reached the summit. It was still morning, and his companions below him were still struggling up the slopes. Yet, on the excuse that they should get back to the river before

dark, Henry Thoreau, the bard of wilderness and untamed nature, turned around and descended.

Safe on the lower slopes, headed toward the lowlands and the
life-giving water, he was able to see human life again as a part
of the great forces of nature, albeit a small part. The experience
at the summit of Katahdin had been overwhelming for him,
though.

"Think of our life in nature," he wrote. "Daily to come in
contact with it — rocks, trees, wind on our cheeks, the solid earth,
the *actual* world. . . . Contact, Contact, who are we? Where are
we?"

11 *Journals in Dreamtime*

 WHEN I RETURNED from Puerto Rico, I found decided changes in the world surrounding the cottage. A warm wind had come up from the south, bringing rain and high winds. The snows had melted back; great flooding puddles were steaming everywhere; and in some south-facing spots in the open meadow I could see, for the first time since December, exposed areas of ground. The grass in these places was a flat, matted brown, and daily, as the south winds held, the brown sections of bare earth expanded. Patches of open forest floor appeared in the woodlands; the path down to the house cleared; and one warm day, not far from the stone wall on the northern side of the property, I saw a mourning cloak butterfly, a hibernating species which commonly emerges in early March.

After that, with a few setbacks, winter began to roll toward spring with a surprising normality. The snowbanks grew smaller and smaller until finally there were only a few deep banks lingering and steaming in the dank, dripping woods. The mourning cloaks began flying regularly; mayflies and obscure woodland insects appeared in the air. The red-winged blackbirds returned on schedule early in March, and then a few days later, coming home along the Great Road, not far from the Digital Equipment plant, I saw a flight of grackles.

One day toward the end of the month the wind veered around

to the southwest again and clouds moved in, bringing with them a heavy downpour. It rained hard all day. Some sections of Beaver Brook rose; a few streets in the area flooded; and at nightfall, with the rain still sheeting down, I went to look for frogs and salamanders.

My daughter and I drove over to a swamp on the west side of the ridge about half a mile from my house. During the first warm, rainy nights of spring I would often see a variety of amphibians there, including the blue-spotted salamander, an endangered species. Finding an endangered animal so close to home, and observing the mad, amphibian frenzy of calling frogs and migrating salamanders always gave me a feeling of hope. But that night I noticed some deep, muddy tracks on the gravel road that led to the swamp, and a curious lack of frogs; usually on such a night they would be everywhere. At the site of the swamp I found out the reason. There was an official sign posted by the road indicating that the area was about to be developed. Behind the sign was an acre or so of raw fill. The wetland itself was gone; the red maples, the reeds and rushes, the sensitive fern, royal fern, and the black alder, the toads, frogs, and salamanders were nowhere to be seen.

We got out of the car to listen. Ordinarily on rainy nights at the end of March this part of the world would be loud with the ringing call of spring peepers. That night there was an ominous stillness, punctuated by the lonely dripping of rain from the surrounding trees, and in the distance the barely perceptible whine of a car.

"Let's go," I said to Lelia. "Nothing left."

We got back in the car and I started it up and turned on the headlights. At the edge of the woods, just inside the trees by the side of the road beyond the swamp, I thought I saw a hunched figure standing in some alders. It looked like a huge bird, a crow, or an owl, its head pulled low, but it was the size of a man, and as soon as the lights flicked on, it stepped backwards into the deeper tangle of the shrubs.

"Go," Lelia said. "Quick. I don't like this."

"It might be old Bill come back again," I said.

"Go," she said.

I pulled forward a little and tried to maneuver the lights into the deeper woods. Far back in the gloom I thought I saw him again, standing perfectly still this time.

"Go," Lelia insisted.

"All right. We're going. But what if that's poor old Bill alone and wet?"

"I don't care. What if it isn't him, and anyway I don't like Bill."

"You don't know Bill, Lelia. He disappeared before you were ever born."

"I still don't like him. Go."

I backed the car around and we drove to the cottage in silence, having failed to hear any frogs or see any salamanders.

"Maybe you're right, Lelia. Maybe that wasn't Bill."

"It wasn't," she said. "It was someone else. And I didn't like him."

Development notwithstanding, the skunk cabbages and the false hellebore poked up in the surviving swamps, and one night, in a clearing in the woodland between my cottage and Beaver Brook, I heard the familiar call of breeding woodcocks. On the twenty-seventh of March the weather cleared. The air was sharper, and it had that rich, lush odor of moist earth and early spring. From the little patch of woodland just north of my house I could hear the familiar call of a phoebe. I was not surprised. Phoebes are seen elsewhere in the region earlier than that date, but they always come to my land on the twenty-seventh of March, no matter what. The newly arrived bird scouted around the land for a week or so, and then later, after a mate appeared, the two of them built a nest in the shed my brother and I had built behind my house. As the weather warmed, I watched them raise their young.

One March some years earlier I was doing research at the

library of the Harvard Museum of Comparative Zoology. I was looking for photographs by William Brewster, a Concord ornithologist who, during the late nineteenth century, had photographed the landscape west of Boston. While we were poking around, the librarian pulled a notebook from the stacks. "Look at these," she said casually. "Thoreau's notes." I opened it. I remember a certain charge or tingling sensation as soon as I saw the scrawly penmanship of the man who lived at Walden Pond. Scanning the month of March, my eyes fell on the notation for the twenty-seventh. There, in his rolling hand, he had noted that the phoebe had arrived that morning.

The same librarian told me on another occasion that it was not Brewster who had taken most of the photographs I was so interested in but a black man named W. S. Gilbert, or simply Gilbert. I knew this name. In many of the Brewster photographs there is a youngish black man, finely dressed, who appears in company with some of Brewster's Boston acquaintances. I learned that Gilbert was his manservant, a sort of jack-of-all-trades who accompanied him everywhere and was popular with Brewster's rich friends. The librarian explained that Brewster would point his stick at a scene that he wanted to record, and the resourceful Gilbert would go about the picky business of setting up the cumbersome nineteenth-century camera to take the photo. This would explain how it was that William Brewster managed to appear in his own shots.

Brewster spent part of his summers and many of his weekends at his country estate, October Farm, in Concord. Some nights he would sleep at a camp, or cabin, on the Concord River about a mile below his house. He had landscaped the woods around the cabin with wildflowers, which he, his workers, and his friends would dig up from the surrounding woodlands. He also had a strange tomblike boathouse on the river where he kept canoes and other small craft for outings with his friends.

One day I walked down a long dirt road to the spot on the river where the cabin and the boathouse and gardens once stood.

Just off the road about a quarter-mile from the cabin site was an eighteenth-century gambrel-roofed house with a sagging ridgepole and a crumbling chimney. Except for a chain and a dog's water bowl by the front door, the house looked deserted. I threaded my way between the dead cars, passed a sagging barn, and went down the wagon track to the river, where I found the boathouse. There in the cement wall I saw the initials "WB, 1916."

I also searched for the remains of the cabin, but I couldn't find them, and after spending some time beside the river, I decided to go back home. The feeling of time past was almost palpable there. In the wind, in the flow of the river, I imagined I could almost hear the voices of the boating parties that used to launch at this very spot, nearly one hundred years ago. I believe I was able to pick out some of the same trees I had seen in Brewster's photographs.

On the way back to my car that day I first met Sanferd Benson. Not far from the crumbling house with the gambrel roof, I saw an old man who appeared to have materialized from the time of Brewster. He was standing in the middle of the dirt road, dressed in baggy overalls, and he had lank, white hair and circular, cloudy glasses. I introduced myself and told him why I was there. He told me his name, announced that he was ninety years old, and said that both he and his father had been born in that house. I did a quick calculation and figured that his father must have been alive when Brewster was living at October Farm.

"Did your father ever know a man named William Brewster?" I asked him.

"Why, *I* knew William Brewster," he said. "I worked for him when I was a boy, and I will tell you that he was as fine a man as ever walked the earth."

Benson's father had worked as a handyman for Brewster, and Sanferd would regularly help out with the chores. He realized, in retrospect, that Brewster had paid him far more than the going rate.

"He was ever so generous, don't you know. As fine a man as ever walked the earth."

On later visits I discovered that this expression was a favorite of his.

"Mr. Brewster had the darkest eyes of any man as ever walked the earth," he would say. "Mr. Brewster was as kind as any man as ever walked the earth."

The old man was a wealth of knowledge. His memory of the nineteenth century was better than his recollection of events of a few years past, and he had a fine memory for detail.

I asked him if he had ever heard of Gilbert.

"Why, I *knew* Gilbert. He was my age. We used to play together."

He leaned a little closer to me.

"Did you know that Gilbert was one of these 'colored' fellows?" he asked. He said this as if there were perhaps one or two hundred black people in the entire world.

After that day I kept running across Gilbert's name. It seems that after Brewster's death Gilbert, who had become a favorite among the photographer's Boston Brahmin circle, had gone on to college. Benson told me that Gilbert was the first black man to graduate from Harvard.

"He became rich, even," Sanferd explained. "He went over to Stockholm and made a great deal of money making shoe polish. But the war came" (he meant the Great War) "and he couldn't get the fat he needed for his mix, and he lost his fortune."

Periodically over the next few years I would ask Mr. Benson more questions about Gilbert. But the capstone of this arch of events was put in place the winter I lived in my cottage.

As part of my rereading of the classics, I read *Tender Is the Night* that winter. One sleeting Sunday afternoon I came to a passage about the murder of a black man in a Paris hotel. In the course of the investigation an American man named Jules Peterson appears on the scene. He is described as "a small respectable Negro on the suave model." Fitzgerald tells us that

Peterson was from Stockholm, where he had failed as a manu-
facturer of shoe polish. Everything coincided — the year, the
description of the man, the business, the place. Jules Peterson
must have been modeled on Gilbert.

One of the other journals I had acquired that winter was a short
piece of writing begun, coincidentally, in the year that Thoreau
died, 1862. My grandfather was twenty-three at the time and
living in Port Tobacco, Maryland, teaching school. He began his
journal on a whim, in a sort of running contest, as he said, with
a "young lady" of his acquaintance. In contrast to some of the
other journals I was reading that year, this one gave no partic-
ulars of the environment, no sense of place or personal quest.
The journals begin early in the year 1862 and dry up at the
beginning of August that year. What is interesting about them
is what they don't say. The Civil War was swirling through the
countryside around him when he was setting down his notes,
but he makes only oblique references to it. On Ash Wednesday,
March 5, for example, he recalls his college companions of the
year before, "many [of whom] are now engaged in war — perhaps fighting on this very day." On August 5, the last entry in
his journal, he comments on the death of a school companion,
one Mike Robertson: "He fell gallantly fighting at the head of
his company." The journal ends on this note with one of its few
musings: "While in life," he wrote, "we are in the midst of death.
Remember well, the night of death draws near."

Not long after ending the journal my grandfather rowed
across the Potomac at night, avoiding the Yankee gunboats, and
subsequently joined "the Cause" as a noncombatant. He entered
the Virginia Theological Seminary and worked in Confederate
hospitals in the region. During this same period his younger
brother Andrew served in the cavalry with the notorious Mosby
Raiders, the terror of Yankee encampments. I have a photo of
Uncle Andrew in front of Appomatox Court House on the day
of surrender. His horse hangs its head as if in sorrow, and Uncle

Andrew stares defiantly out from beneath his slouch hat with the sharp black eyes that are characteristic of that side of my family.

"Mine is such a small and uneventful life, there is not much to record," Andrew's brother, my grandfather, wrote in his journal during the height of the war.

In sharp contrast to these writings are the journals of my father. He began writing them early in his life, at age sixteen or seventeen, and continued writing until he was forty, when he finally married. The richest of these journals in a personal way are those covering his first year at college, when, in November, his mother died suddenly, followed shortly thereafter by his father, who had been sick for almost a year. But the most interesting historically are the accounts of his three years in China, 1915 to 1918.

The international world of Shanghai, the squalor and the intensity of Chinese life at this period of history, was a shock to my father, accustomed as he was to the small, sleepy life of the Eastern Shore. In the little glimpses I get from his journals, his childhood seems to have been idyllic. He passed his days in autumn scouring the forest with bands of friends, collecting chestnuts or hunting squirrels. In summer he sailed on the bay, swam, took excursions to river farms; and he whiled away the winters with cards and conversation. But in China he was overwhelmed by the colors, the tumultuous crowds, the filth, the smells, and the indifference to life. He was sometimes desperately homesick. The whistle of a steamer in the harbor would flood him with yearnings for the Eastern Shore, and there are times in his journal when the intensity of life in China, the bitter proximity to the edge of total dissolution, was too much; he would leave things out.

He got lost in the countryside one night after returning late from a pheasant-hunting trip on the Grand Canal. He and some companions had taken a canal boat inland, had moored along with hundreds of other boats, and then, having walked across several fields, had proceeded into some woods on the side of a hill. My father became separated from the group; coming back after dark, while he was crossing the fields, he stumbled over something in the middle of plowed land. He does not explain clearly in the journals what it was.

The story of this hunting party became part of family folklore. What he found in the field, he told us, was a "poor dead puppy." This in itself was enough to evoke in us children a deep sense of pity and fear. But in retrospect it seems odd that a man who was certainly used to the death of animals, and who had encountered extremes of destitution in China, should have been so shocked by a dead puppy. It was not until years later, when we were all grown, that he told my brother Hugh that what he had found in the field that night was not a puppy but a dead baby.

Death was all around him in China. Daily bodies would float by on the river. He describes sickly, hungry crowds, lepers with running sores, beggars lining the streets in certain quarters, starvation in the countryside, trains of refugees moving from place to place, flood, famine, and plague. He wrote home mentioning — briefly, as if it were normal — the conditions. The country was on the verge of a dangerous plague, which, for the time being, had not spread beyond Nanking. "But as usual in China, there are other troubles," he wrote. "Thousands are homeless from floods earlier in the year. Dikes have breached and river water has flooded the precious surrounding lowlands, meaning more famine in the coming year." Civil unrest was still raging. "Bandits are worse than usual," he reported. "Recently they captured some American engineers and are holding them for ransom. Conditions in the interior are all terribly unsettled. And yet, life goes on as usual. That is the remarkable thing about China; no matter how unsettled are political matters, you are still able to travel, mail letters, and hold school." Surrounded by this chaos my father began a journal of a different sort.

One night he and a group of his friends became involved in

a discussion of dreams and their meaning. As he explained in the introduction to this new journal, since coming out to China his dreams had been particularly vivid, so he decided to keep a diary of them, "a mere record," as he called it, "of the unrestrained flights of the imagination. It should prove interesting to the future."

This was the pre-Freudian, pre-Jungian era, at least for my father, and what seemed to interest him most was the interrelationship between waking life and the life of dreams. As a result, he recorded on the left-hand page of the journal the account of a dream, and on the right-hand page some possible explanation, most of which had to do with the events of his life at that period.

The accounts of the dreams are quintessential personal journals, a voyage into the unconscious. My father had set out to explore the wider world, but having got there, he seems to have discovered Thoreau's dictum that it is not worth the while to fit out an expedition and sail round the world to count the cats of Zanzibar. He embarked on a voyage to (in Thoreau's words) "that farthest western way, which does not pause at the Mississippi or the Pacific, nor conduct toward a worn out China or Japan." He was headed inward.

In March of 1917 my father began having confused, clamorous dreams. The month's journal opens with a dream of a revolt of the blacks in his hometown. Crowds of ordinarily peaceful people appear on the streets in front of his boyhood home. They are woolly headed and are carrying "bolas" — knifelike weapons which my father says he had never known about until *after* the dream. My father tries to placate them; he talks to them from the porch and asks to see their pistols. Then he tells them about a gun he has, a big army .45. The crowd breaks up.

In another dream he returns to college and there meets an old friend, but the friend for some reason cannot recognize him. His teeth break in one dream. In another he meets his brother — who often appears in the dreams of this period. His brother asks him a question that he cannot understand, and my father replies in Chinese, which his brother cannot comprehend. In another, while holding down the shafts of a rickshaw for some friends, my father is lifted high above the ground and then brought down again with a painless but uncomfortable crash. He dreams that he and his Chinese students are swimming and executing fanciful dives near a waterfall. One of the students is swept over. On the night of March 13 he dreams of an immense building with "wide high flights of white steps." There is confusion in the building; lights are burning in various rooms; stray dogs wander in and out. Somehow he is in charge of the great flight of stairs. On the sixteenth he dreams that "aeroplanes" cover the sky. They turn out to be kites, but while he watches, a real plane flies in among them. A few nights later he is traveling on a steamer. Three bombs explode somewhere on board, and the ship is sunk, but my father manages to get to a rocky wild shore. He is impressed with the vegetation in the tidal pools, and it occurs to him that he may have to eat it to survive on this island. But then, in the way of dreams, he sees civilized people, one of whom he knows, who are swimming and having tea.

On the right-hand page of this dream diary the record of his daily life helps only with the superficialities of his dreams. He uses real people, places, and events as cast and setting; the plays remain deeply symbolic. War was surging around him in those years: the civil unrest in China, the Great War in Europe, and the Russian Revolution. Ships were sinking, bombs were exploding, and things did appear to be falling apart. One night he dreams that he is a child again, at home in Centreville, in bed. His father comes in and explains that he has been in a sporting event with the Kaiser. His father struck the Kaiser, and then later the Kaiser appeared in full military uniform, demanding an apology, which his father refused to grant. On the right-hand page of the diary my father writes that in Shanghai they were waiting daily for news of the impending outbreak of war with Germany. During this same period he dreams of revolutions in Russia and Germany. Crowds surge into streets demanding democracy. He dreams again of crowds in Centreville.

There are certain recurrent symbols in my father's dreams; one is the presence of a large empty house, another is the presence of dogs — they are forever wandering in and out of his interior landscapes. Early in March he dreams that he is exploring such a house with his mother, who, as he points out on the right-hand page, was not living at the time of the dream. He and his mother wander through the house and, on the third floor, come to a succession of small bedrooms with beautiful mahogany beds and fine counterpanes. The rooms are notable for their extreme neatness and the absence of other furniture. In time they come to another series of rooms and to a window. From this window there is a magnificent view: "A great lowland country stretched away to a wonderful serried mountain chain which was partly obscured by mist. At the foot of the mountains there stood a splendid city." He can tell by the minarets and graceful domes that the city is Constantinople. Some of the buildings appear to be gold.

He had never seen Constantinople, but he had been reading the night before of a mountain in the Cévennes (Pic de Finiels) with the Mediterranean in the far distance (he was probably reading Stevenson's *Travels with a Donkey*). Late in the month — coincidentally on the same date on which, fifty years later, he would die — he experienced what seems to have been the most significant of all of these strange dreams.

He finds himself again inside one of his great buildings, complete with wandering stray dogs This time he and a number of people are somehow locked in. He manages to get a door open and begins to search for a way out, but encounters instead more corridors that seem to lead nowhere. Finally, he comes to a large room that is lined with a series of doorways. Each door is shut, and on each are written illegible words. But one door has a lamp beside it and the lettering here is quite clear. The door is marked "The Room of Death."

My father is very curious about this room; he wants to look

in but is afraid. Then suddenly a girl with light hair appears and prevents him from entering. Seeing her he feels a deep contentment, and he asks her if she has a message for him. She leans toward him intimately. "You must know," she says. "I would not have come here if I did not care for you."

Not long after this the dream journal becomes sporadic, and finally, after a few post-China entries, ceases altogether.

The journals of Henry Thoreau, which some consider his best work, concern themselves not so much with personal matters as with the three great themes of his life — the mystic quest, the study of natural history, and the business of living well. There are moments when, in an oblique way — in a manner almost designed to lay itself open to interpretation by future biographers — Henry records some of his feelings. In particular there are the passages dealing with his relationship with Ellen Sewall. He also sets down, from time to time, his recurrent dreams. One is his account of the rough and the smooth, a dream in which, at one moment, he finds himself lying on a very uncomfortable, rough surface somehow associated with death. Shortly thereafter he is on a smooth surface, very pleasing to the touch. Another, perhaps more significant dream is a recurrent vision of a mountain top. This is a wonderfully universal dream, clearly related to the spiritual heights symbolized by mountains and to the experiences that he had on Katahdin and on other climbs.

In the dream he must work his way up through a dark and unfrequented wood at the base of the mountain. Slowly, as he ascends, the trees begin to thin, and he emerges onto a rocky ridge with stunted trees and wild beasts. Finally he loses himself in the upper air and clouds and achieves a summit that is somehow above the earthly line, which has a "superterranean grandeur and sublimity." "You are lost the minute you set foot there," he writes. "You know no path, but wander thrilled, over the bare pathless rock, as if it were solidified air and cloud."

This dream, which he had at least twenty times, seems to

prefigure his ascent of Katahdin. There he struggled up through a dark forest and across a rocky stretch where the trees were stunted, and where, as he imagined at least, bears lurked in their dens below him. Finally he entered into a kingdom of clouds and air, a sublime swirling universe where everything was obscured.

Given the metaphor, it is little wonder that Henry turned around on Katahdin and, without ever achieving the actual summit, descended to his friends. To go on would have been death.

Henry's dream mountain seems to have been located on a hill just east of Concord Center — in the same place where the village burying ground is found — and it is little wonder that he should have used such a place in the landscape of his dreams. The association of heights and the afterlife seems fairly clear.

I have had, over the years, a recurrent dream that is in exact opposition to the ascendant dreams of Henry Thoreau and the wide steps and vistas of which my father dreamed. My dreams are pre-Christian and classical: I descend into the underworld, into the surreal architecture of the Paris Métro and the New York subways, where, unfortunately, I have spent more time than I would like. Here in the half-lit subterranean world, trains come and go carrying passengers; crowds move silently and determinedly; and around me, ascending and descending, are moving stairs on which people stand patiently. Tracks run above and below; there are many platforms, ticket counters, and turnstiles; and of course I am lost in the midst of these labyrinthine tunnels. My quest there is to get on the right train and thereby, like Orpheus, get back into the upper world.

In the way of dreams, the place is very familiar to me even though I am lost. I make my way through the passages and turnstiles into a well-lighted car that deposits me at a wide station platform, emptied of crowds. Here, at the very end of the platform, is a narrow stairway with light spilling down from the other world. I walk to the stairway and ascend. Even though this dream often begins in Paris, when I finally break out into the upper streets I am invariably in New York — oddly enough, somewhere in the Bronx. But this is not the city of dark canyons, wandering gangs, and derelict buildings. It is a semiwilderness, a wide landscape where the sun is shining and a fresh wind is blowing.

That March in my cottage I had a similar dream involving trains. The day before I had the dream was one of those abnormally warm March days, when the ground virtually oozes, when mourning cloak butterflies appear, and the song sparrows and redwings seem to call with more intensity than usual. I took a walk late in the morning, following the same route I had taken on skis during the winter, and ended up in the parking lot of the Digital plant.

I was still getting nowhere in my attempts to gain entry into LKP 595. I had received no official response to my requests to visit the place, even though I had, as instructed, humbly submitted them in writing. I would call from time to time to find out how my case was faring, but the public relations officials were rarely able to come to the phone, and none returned my calls. Once or twice I did get through and was assured that my case had been "pitched," but that the possibilities of talking to managers or engineers inside LKP 595 were slim.

The difficulties of obtaining an audience simply whetted my curiosity, and the mystery of the plant began to grow in my mind. The building began to seem ominous, and although I knew that Digital Equipment was among the most humane of large corporations, the secrecy of the place, the chain link fence, the ever-searching TV surveillance, and the seeming impenetrability of the structure combined to create in my imagination a dark cathedral dedicated to some nefarious god. I could not help but think of a book published by the friend of a friend of mine. His thesis was that the computer is the embodiment of Ahriman, the dark overlord of early Zoroastrians, who has returned in electronic form and is living inside the computers of the world, attempting to spread evil.

The TV surveillance cameras of Ahriman and his minions paid no attention to me that March day as I crossed the Digital parking lot. They searched blindly, indifferent to my presence. Just as I was about to return home, I saw a man in cowboy clothes with a beard and shoulder-length hair getting into an old Saab. It occurred to me that if I were ever to gain entry into LKP 595 it would be through personal rather than corporate contact, so I went over to him and explained my mission.

I had found the right person. He turned out to be not only friendly and talkative but also an old line "Deccy," as the long-time Digital workers refer to themselves. In spite of his appearance, he was rather highly placed in the company, and although he was at first slightly skeptical, he said that he might be able to show me around sometime, but that he would have to think about it a little, since employees were not supposed to admit simply any stranger. I think I convinced him of my ignorance — and my innocence. As I explained to him, I barely knew what software was. We exchanged telephone numbers, and I promised to call him in a week or so.

That night I had a Digital dream. In the background of the dream there stood the great flat cathedral, dark windows absorbing the light. But somewhere in front of the building, on my side of the valley, there was a small trolley with open cars. The employees of the corporation sat obediently in neat rows while the train carried them across the valley to their place of work. I boarded the train, and then I noticed the ticket taker and driver (or engineer). He was a large man, ever so polite, and without looking up, and in an entirely businesslike way, he took my ticket and turned to the controls to start the train. I recognized the driver the minute I saw him: it was the "engineer" Kenny Olsen.

Before I took my seat, I looked back along the length of the train. The workers were all sitting in their proper places, waiting. Then I saw that the last car was only half-filled, and far in the back, in the last seat, which ran all the way across the back of the car, there sat an odd-looking individual. In contrast to the brightly clad Digital workers, he was dressed in a gray-brown suit, a white shirt, and a black silk bow tie. He was small, had thick, light brown hair and was sitting with his legs crossed, with one arm thrown irreverently across the back seat. At first I thought he was staring directly at me with his intense gray-blue eyes, but then I realized he was looking beyond me at the driver of the train, Kenny Olsen. The man in gray had a sort of cynical, resigned smirk on his face as if to say, "You see, I knew it would come to this." I recognized him immediately too: it was Henry Thoreau.

12 The Cruelest Month

ON THE TWELFTH of April a great congress of crows collected in the white pine trees just west of the stone wall by the meadow. They gathered not long after dawn and set up a racket that woke me immediately. The noise increased; little groups would rise above the trees, hover, settle, rise again, and beat their wings madly, cawing all the while. I made coffee and carried a cup out to the terrace, but as soon as I sat down, the congress came to some obscure decision and moved on. A huge shouting wave of crows rose above the trees and streamed down the open meadow, crossed the road, and disappeared into the old fields below the house. Somewhere down by the flood plains of Beaver Brook they settled again. I could hear them cawing in the distance, their voices rising and falling in the morning air.

There is something tremendously evocative for me in the calling of a flock of crows. When I was young I used to spend summers on my uncle's farm in Maryland. The Eastern Shore is good country for crows — wide stretches of corn and grain fields interspersed with tall groves of hardwoods for roosting. Every summer morning I would be awakened by their raucous calling and see the rolling flocks wavering over distant fields. To this day the sound of flocks making up at dawn brings memories of open summer windows, the smell of rural dawn, and fresh-cut hay.

I had been thinking a lot about Maryland, since I had not only been reading my father's accounts of his childhood there, but also rereading the journals of a landholding cousin of mine who spent most of his life on the Eastern Shore, a man who, although talented in a number of fields, seemed to prefer obscurity. Doctor John, as he was called locally, actively sought the small life.

John died unexpectedly one afternoon in spring after returning from one of his frequent nature walks. He came into the house, announced that he was tired, took off his boots, and lay down on his favorite couch. He was found four hours later, at peace, finally. After the funeral, people stayed on at his house, nosing through his possessions, and I happened to find his nature journals, the one record he kept of his life. Those few days I read over sections of them, trying to find some key to the man. Of all my older cousins, of whom there are many on the Eastern Shore, he was the one I appreciated the most and understood the least. I used to take walks with him sometimes and in fact had walked with him one spring day not long before his death.

Each spring my brother Jim makes a pilgrimage to the Eastern Shore, where he stays with family and friends, visits my father's grave, and wanders around various former family holdings and shrines paying homage to a way of life that ended for my family in the 1930s, when my parents left Maryland for good. Since I was myself delving into the past through my journal reading, I decided to leave my cottage and go with him that April.

I drove to Jim's house in Connecticut, and the next day we went down to Easton and stayed on a boat belonging to one of Jim's many women friends. It was still cold on the water and the boat was unheated, but we slept there for a few nights and wandered the countryside by day. The second day we visited my cousins in Centreville, who lived in the house where my father was born. They told us yet again the stories about the Eastern Shore that we had heard in our childhood, a slow, almost sacred litany of the places and the people that were the foundation of the family that we were once a part of. We also visited the farm where Doctor John had lived.

The place had changed hands by this time, so my brother and I drove down to the river bank to a house next to John's property, a house where I had spent a summer with my parents the year I was fourteen. From there, skirting the marshy shores of the Chester River, we walked down to John's. Above us on the hill we could see the old river house, its formal front door, as with all the eighteenth-century dwellings in these parts, facing not the road but the river, where all the traffic passed in those times.

We began to climb toward the house, discreetly staying out of sight. On the way up the hill we passed a little spur road where I had last walked with Doctor John one March day back in the 1960s. He and I had gone down to the river to catch the glinting afternoon light and watch the packs of geese gather on the bay beyond the point. There was a wind coming off the water, and as soon as we stepped from the shelter of the woods into the stubble of the corn field, it spilled across his forehead, loosing a few strands of gray hair. Crows in the bare trees behind us gabbled among themselves, holding their wings out like paper kites about to lift off. There were foxes in the ground, and fox squirrels and fox sparrows in the woods, and the air was saturated with the rank smell of moist soil. In the distance we could hear the yelp of the geese, and we could see them far beyond the fields, a patch of moist gray, the color of December. Once, standing near here, John and I saw a huge raft of swans and geese rise up from the river and settle somewhere beyond the point. The flock was so immense that the vanguard had landed before those at the rear had even taken wing. The result was a huge arc of gray bodies and wings in the air, a long, resounding bridge that stretched over the bay. John said the flocks were like fugues, like intertwining themes. He loved music — the long line of the cello, the sound of the leaves scuttling at his doorstep, the call of geese, and the summer bark of bullfrogs in the pond on the inland side of his property. People used to say he thought too much.

He and I had hiked along the tractor road beside the woods with the corn field on our right and the river below us. It was here, or at least not far from here, that I had discovered a family of fox kits wrestling at the edge of the corn the summer I was ten. They were so deeply engaged in fighting, so intent on getting a better bite at the neck of a sibling, that they did not notice me standing there, my heart pounding. When I got back to the house I told John, who listened in his steady way, nodding, but said nothing. He paced himself; he took his time; he watched things.

There was something almost scriptural about his journal keeping. He recorded the passage of the natural world as if he were its manager, as if failure to do so would mean the dissolution of his universe. The journal was meticulous, filled with wind direction, temperature, and minute accounts of bird nests, insect hatchings, and the tonality of calling frogs. There was not a word there about personal pain. But rereading his journals fifteen years after his death, I saw intimations of his demise written there. He was feeling more toward the end, or he was allowing himself to feel.

Uncommon birds had moved in the winter before he died, northern species that in ordinary winters would not have come so far south. Huge flocks of redpolls had been seen gleaning the tree tops at the woods' edge. There were fast-moving flights of winter finches, crossbills, and grosbeaks, and tiny packs of whispering siskins. The robins stayed north in inordinate numbers, the juncos were abundant everywhere, and out on the river the great arcs of swans and geese rose and settled like dreamscape architecture. "The winter is charged," he wrote with unusual eloquence, "the seasons turned upside down."

By February of that year he was speculating about the curious winter. Some of the older people said that it was a bad year down at Pea Island on the Outer Banks, that food was scarce, and so the waterfowl had stayed north. They said food was also scarce in Canada and New England. There were deep freezes that year on the mainland and a dearth of pine cones. The world was bleak, ironbound, but the sea and the bays and the rivers mellowed the peninsula. The rye stayed green in the fields, the woods were open, and the swamps were dank and smelled of skunk cabbage.

Uncharacteristically he began reminiscing with his friends. He also took to wandering. Betsy, his housekeeper, said later that he was rising earlier than usual, leaving the house in the pitch dark. He would spend whole days in the field, binoculars on his chest, his eternal notebook in the loose pockets of his jacket. Once or twice he did not appear for dinner. Betsy heard him come in around ten.

John had served in two world wars; he was very young in the first one and had had a nasty time in the trenches, according to local gossip — something about a cave-in and buried men, voices from the mud. In the second war he was a doctor with the medical corps in Europe, and later in India. I know only one thing about his time in India. One night as he was returning to his encampment through a forested area, a tiger jumped onto the hood of his jeep and remained there, staring at him through the windshield, the full moon gleaming in its eyes.

It was the only story he would tell from his war years.

"What happened after that?" we always asked, even though we had heard the story many times before.

"He glared at me. Pale green eyes in the white light of the moon. And then, slowly, and don't ask me why, I stood up in the open jeep, one leg on the seat, and I looked at him over the windscreen. I could smell meat on his breath and muddy paws."

"And then?" we would ask. We always had to push for the ending.

"And then he raised himself up slowly, ever so slowly, he leaned forward . . ."

We nodded enthusiastically.

"And then, sniffing, he touched my nose with his. Actually touched my nose, as a dog would."

The song sparrows and the fox sparrows came back early that spring. The skunk cabbage and the false hellebore unfolded early in the swamps, and the winter finches lingered on so that they mixed with the returning flocks of sparrows, robins, and blackbirds. There was almost too much activity to record in his journals. He would walk the fields along the woods' edge listening to the gabbling and the whistles, the chirps and the fluttering of the birds.

It was early in March that year that I had taken my last walk with him. We left his house on one of those freakish early spring days. The air was almost palpable with moisture and life, the water smell filling every dip and low spot in the fields and woods, and the sun angling through the ground mists as through cathedral windows. We found the body of a freshly killed wood duck near a wooded swamp. It was in full plumage, and it seemed a shame to me that such a thing of beauty should perish in such a hopeful season. I said as much.

"It's all right," he said. "This is a good day to die."

We walked on for a while in silence, toward the river where the flocks were gathering again.

"The Sioux used to say that before they would go into battle," he said. "I've always thought it made a lot of sense, to simply decide to die on some good day."

In his youth he used to hunt, but he quit when he came back from the first war. They said he would sometimes go down to the blind alone with a dog and a gun, but he would always return empty-handed.

"I'm waiting for the perfect moment," he would argue.

When he came back from the second war, he didn't even bother to make the trip to the blind. He moved to New York, worked at a city hospital, and then retired early.

By the middle of the month the spring migration was in full

force, but the winter finches had still not left, and the flocks of geese and swans had stayed late into the season. That spring in front of the drug store in the town where the old men gathered, they commented on it. Some said the world had gone dry beyond the peninsula. An old black man who lived behind the ice house began walking the streets ranting at people, as he sometimes did. "It's the red moon," he shouted at passersby. "The striped moon."

Doctor John would stay up late at night writing in his journals. Regularly he would leave the house before dawn, return after dark for dinner, and then retire to his study to write. He reveled in the early unfolding of the flowers and the greening of the fields.

I remember an autograph book my parents had kept since the early forties. House guests and various family members had signed it with comments in little columns set down for autobiographical material. Doctor John had signed it in April 1948. Under a heading marked "Likes" he had written, "Birds, trees, green grass." And then farther down in the column, separate from the other notations, "A simple life."

In New York after the Second World War he had married. She was a society woman who liked the out-of-doors and shocked the local Eastern Shore people with her eccentric style. She loved to cut hay and could often be seen in the fields driving a tractor in her flowered dress. Often she and John would disappear to her family's hunting camp in the Adirondacks, where they would climb mountains, swim nude, it was rumored, and study nature. She died at an early age and left him without issue.

By the time he was seventy-five years old he had filled fourteen books of nature notes without telling us anything except that the world was a very orderly place in which birds returned at the appointed season, in which the grass would green up on the same date every year, in which the frogs called from the swamps each in its proper season, in which the turtles laid their eggs, the geese departed or returned, the swans grouped and regrouped, and the natural system functioned in a seemingly eternal cycle.

"But you didn't finish the tiger story," I said to him.

"It touched my nose," he continued.

There was an immense flock of blackbirds in the forest to our left, and when he spoke they rose in a body and began wheeling over the woods, gathering more birds as they circled.

"It leaned forward and touched my nose and I could feel the dank wetness of it."

Out on the river the light went silver for a moment, then turned a warm summer yellow. The swans and geese began talking.

"Then it drew back cautiously. It turned and jumped from the hood and sauntered down the middle of the road away from the jeep. Casually, you understand, no hurry. It cut into the forest and then came back; its head appeared from a thicket beside the jeep. I could see the white whiskers, a face striped like the moon."

The blackbirds broke from their gyre and flowed in a curling wave down over the corn field. The song sparrows and the fox sparrows set up a loud chatter as they moved among the trees, and out on the river the great flocks shifted, barking and yelping among themselves. The noise of the land birds suddenly intensified; the geese and swans increased their calling. He noticed. I saw him swing his head quickly. There was a look that I had never seen in his eyes, a hint of fear perhaps. Then he looked at me directly, as directly as he ever had in all my life with him.

"It spoke to me, you know. Maybe I was under pressure. Maybe I only imagined it, but I'm certain it spoke to me. I can't forget that. I have lived with it all these years."

Under the sweet gum woods there was a sudden rush of wind. The birds went silent. The river opened; the arrow flight of ducks fell; the geese and the swans pumped and backfilled to stillness. A cloud shifted, and out on the river the light flared with silver.

They buried him in April. He was old, and not many were left to cry at his funeral.

I put in another garden later that month. While I was digging out a long strip along the west wall, I uncovered an old mouse-gnawed horse bone, the last of the wild white horse that George Case used to ride in the days when the meadow was an orchard. I turned under a load of cow manure that I had got from the farm beyond the west side of the ridge, and then I limed and raked, and when the soil was warm enough, I planted roses and herb borders, snapdragons, cosmos, peonies, stock, and sweet peas. I had it in mind to create a little corner of civilization, a place to take tea on a summer afternoon.

In contrast to Henry Thoreau, who felt oppressed by the cultivated fields and dooryard gardens of his area, I felt that my small part of the world still needed a little more cultivation. The deep, wild forest, so beloved by Henry, was all around me, threatening to jump into my meadow. The woods were rank and tangled with fallen limbs, dead trees, dark, moist hollows where insects danced in cool shafts of light. I loved the dark, wooded mystery of the ridge, but I felt the need for a middle ground between the chaos of the human industrial community and the wilderness of nature, a place where the refinements rather than the brute economic force of human endeavor could be experienced.

The garden progressed slowly, as gardens always do in New England in the spring. Cold rains came, a snow flurry or two; the soil was dampened again and unworkable, and I returned to my wood fire to think and read. Spring is such a hopeful season in theory, but in fact it is filled with loss. It is no wonder, as statistics indicate, that more people lose ground and succumb in this season than in any other. In the histories of the people I had known and loved I saw not the rebirth that Henry claimed to experience in spring but the other side of life, which is death.

Doctor John died in spring, and so did my father. So did Henry, for that matter.

Three years before his death, and not long after his retirement, my father signed on as chaplain for a Dutch cruise ship that was headed around the world. Although he was a seasoned traveler, he seems to have worried a great deal about this trip. In mid-Atlantic, on the outbound voyage, he developed an ulcer and had to be hospitalized, and when the ship reached Cannes, he was put ashore and sent to a small French hospital not far from Nice. Somebody had to go and bring him home, and since I had lived for a while in Nice and spoke French, my family sent me, even though I was the youngest.

It was a curious week for me. I had, for once, the money to rent a room in a decent hotel, but instead stayed with friends in the cheaper district at the back side of the city. At night I would return to some of the old cafés I had known; by day I would take the bus west to the hospital. It was the most pleasant hospital I have ever visited — small, with high ceilings, polished wood floors, and landscaped grounds. My father was in a west-facing ground-floor room with French doors that opened onto a terrace, and as soon as I arrived each day, I would swing open the doors and let the fresh April air of the Mediterranean sweep in. I would spend the day with my father, translating if necessary, talking to him, or sitting in the sun just beyond the door. When he recovered enough to make the flight, I shepherded him to the airport and we flew on to Barcelona, and then across the Atlantic to New York.

There was some heavy weather on that trip. Just after the noonday meal was served, the plane began to hit rolling pockets of air that roughed us up considerably, and at one point we hit a real downdraft. The bottom seemed to fall out of the sky; the plane dropped straight down for several seconds and then came up with a jerk. I looked over and noticed that my father had stopped eating and was staring straight ahead, his eyes fixed on some singular point in front of him. I asked him if everything was all right, but he couldn't answer. I noticed that he was gripping the armrests of his seat. I think I was a little surprised that such an experienced traveler should be so terrified, although I realize now that he simply knew more than I; I was too young to be scared.

Some years earlier, my middle brother, Hugh, the aspiring poet, who had a way of living on the very edge of things, had finally cracked up at college. My father had to bring him home to rest. On the flight back they too hit some heavy weather, and my father had the same reaction. My brother took the opportunity to question my father's faith. "If you believe," he said, "you should have nothing to fear." My father simply stared straight ahead.

While he was on shipboard he needed a transfusion. A male nurse on the trip, a Dutchman, donated his blood. Three years later my father came down with hepatitis, picked up, the doctors said, from that transfusion. He got sick in midwinter and was hospitalized in March. While he was in the hospital my brothers and I entertained him by reading news stories about China. But then he grew delirious, went into a coma, and, after three days, died. It was the first day of spring. Just before he went into the coma, while I was sitting with him, he had a moment of lucidity and mumbled something about the father and the son. I never knew whether he was talking about family or Christianity.

Henry seems to have become more comfortable with death by the time he moved to Walden. The theory of the necessity of death for the regeneration of life was in evidence all around him — in the woods, the pond, and the fields. The thawing earth, the melting ice, and the return of the green grass and birds was a strong metaphor for him. It was almost as if he saw the earth as a living thing itself, which, like all living things, would die but was capable of regeneration. While he was living in his cabin at Walden he wrote his first book, *A Week on the Concord and Merrimack Rivers,* which is, among other things, an extended paean to his beloved brother. The writing of this work seems to have served as expiation for him, and by the time he was at work on the book *Walden,* the natural rebirth of the cycle of the year was a model for the rebirth of the soul and the continuity of human existence. His passage in *Walden* on the return of life to the winter landscape is one of the most lyrical in the book. Walker that he was, he must have sensed firsthand the freedom that one experiences in New England after the deep snows melt and a person can finally stretch out in a good stride.

"The earth is not a mere fragment of dead history," he wrote in *Walden* ". . . but living poetry like the leaves of trees, which precede flowers and fruits, not a fossil earth, but a living earth.

"So our human life but dies down to its root, and still puts forth its green blade to eternity."

It was perhaps a useful philosophy for a man who would outlive his brother and his older sister, a man who would watch his father die, and who would, in the month of May, at the relatively young age of forty-five, himself die down to the bare root.

13 The Sea of Milk

ONE BRIGHT DAY that spring I went down to see Sanferd Benson. I found him sitting in the sun in the alcove of his old house, resting between chores. He looked frailer than ever. He had turned ninety-five that spring, was decidedly more fragile, and his eyeglasses, which never were in very good shape, had nearly clouded over; he had wired and taped them together at so many points that it was difficult to say exactly what material they had been constructed of in the first place. It occurred to me that he might be legally blind.

"Good day to rest," I said, after the usual reintroductions.

"I rest more and more now, I'm afraid. I don't know why exactly. But at my age I suppose one gets tired."

He was sitting in an old wooden kitchen chair, and he indicated that I should sit down on a crate in the alcove next to him.

"I'm not anxious to split any more wood," he said. "The weather's so fine, and I wonder if I'll see another winter."

That year he had adopted a little dog, a rounded, black and white thing of indeterminate parentage with a pug nose and a short tail. The dog was devoted to him; she followed him wherever he went and would curl up at his feet whenever we stood talking for any length of time. Now she jumped up on his lap and licked his hand while he rubbed her head.

We went over a few of the old stories about William Brewster, and then I asked whether, after ninety years of living in the same place, he felt that he had missed anything.

"Oh my, no," he said enthusiastically. "There was ever so much going on right here, don't you know, with Mr. Brewster and his Cambridge friends. And there was always so much work to do and always so much to look at. You know, new birds have been coming to this land here. I saw a beautiful gray one the other day, with a long tail and these black and white bands on its wings. And there's a little nuthatch with his helmet; and those crested grays, as I call them."

"Titmice," I said.

"Yes, titmice."

He scratched the dog's ears for a while, and looked at her head.

"I'll take a photograph of her someday if you like," I said.

"That would be nice. She's a good girl."

He nodded toward the river. "It's been five years since I've been down to the place where Mr. Brewster had his boathouse. I must go down someday."

"It's in ruins now."

"I know. It was once a fine building, and there were fine people there. Days like this in spring they would come. Father and I would have the boats varnished by then, and they would bring their sandwiches and baskets of cold chicken. Gilbert would go with them. He was a fine rower. You know, all the ladies liked Gilbert, even though he was young."

"I'll have to go down there again and look around."

"There was ever so much to do here. Still is. There's no end, it seems — the woods, the river, these new birds. And I wonder about these newer houses I've heard about up Ball's Hill Road.

"There is a lot to look at."

"You know, I went to Lawrence once, on one of those new highways. But I shan't go there again. There's so much right here. But then I wonder if it isn't all up here."

He tapped the side of his head.

"It's just what you make of a place. What you think it is. Not so much what it really is," he said.

"Sounds true."

"Such an odd thought, really. I've never had such an odd thought."

Later in May I went back to his house with a camera to take pictures of his dog. It was another one of those brilliant days, and Sanferd was in better form this time, working in his strawberry patch. He had a wheelbarrow with him, and as usual the little dog was at his feet. I took a few pictures of him with the dog, but he was stiff and formal, so I began to snap the dog by herself in the harsh spring light.

"Get up here in the wheelbarrow," he said to the dog.

She obediently jumped into the bed and sat down, but she was nervous. He stepped to the side out of the frame. She looked over at him, licking her lips. I took a picture.

"Look at the camera, Muffin," he said.

She shifted, glanced at me, and looked again at Sanferd. I took a few more pictures.

"I'll come back and give them to you in a week or so," I said.

I finished the roll and got the prints back in a few days. There was the dog, her black and white fur shining in the spring light. In the best picture she was looking loyally at her master, who was standing outside the photograph, the dark streak of his shadow passing over her. But before I could deliver the prints, I learned from the local newspaper that the owner of the shadow was dead.

By May the garden that I had planted in April began to consume more and more of my time. The seedlings sprang up out of the moist earth, and neat rows of planted annuals ran along the back wall in orderly, pleasing lanes. They contrasted sharply with the disordered forest held at bay behind the wall. The tentative blossoms of the spring perennials appeared, and all around me in the fields and woods there was a freshening greenness. Great waves of migratory birds rolled up from the south, plunged against a cold front that first week of May, and then, when the weather finally broke, surged over New England, filling the world with song. Long before dawn I could hear them; little whines and chips, whistles and buzzes, burst out from the wall edges and the tree tops, sounds I had not heard in a year — the combined voice of spring. Leaves appeared in the woodland behind the cottage, a small, delicately shaded tracery. Foxes crossed my meadow; and in the old field just north of my house, a fat woodchuck emerged from its burrow and sat alone under the clear sky, squat like a Buddha, meditative and all-knowing. I turned more garden soil, hoed down the channeled rows, planted more flowers, and waited.

Periodically as I worked the soil I would come across more remnants of the Case family, bits of broken dishes and cups, the arm of a China doll, and pieces of old leather shoes. Fifty years ago when old man Case carried his trash up from his house to this spot in the former orchard, he could have looked out and seen the lonely peak of Mount Wachusett to the southwest and the higher peak of Monadnock to the northwest. The land beyond the boundary wall of his property was all cleared field, and if he had cared to, he could have climbed to this spot each evening and watched the sun set over the Schooly Penaplain to the west. In my time the view of Wachusett is obscured by pine and oak forest, but from the other side of the valley, on the rise where the Digital plant now stands, the mountain is still in view, a lonely blue height.

In his time Henry Thoreau could see Wachusett from Concord, and he felt a certain affinity with the mountain. As he pointed out in an early poem, it stood alone, like Henry himself, "without society." For years he and his brother, John, had thought about climbing Wachusett, but had chosen, in their 1839 mountain trip, to go north to the greater heights of the White Mountains. The year John died, Henry decided finally to take the expedition to Wachusett. He and Richard Fuller, the brother of Margaret Fuller, walked there from Concord, climbed to the summit, and spent the night there in a tent. They both kept journals of the trip, and as they walked west they quoted passages about the great journeys and adventures of the heroes of classical Greece. This was a literary trip if there ever was one. Throughout the journal and the subsequent essay that emerged from the walk, Henry quotes from Virgil and Wordsworth. Even after he and his companion retired to the tent, they read their classics by moonlight. It is no wonder Henry tended to see the world as metaphor.

While they were on Wachusett, Henry and Richard Fuller looked north to Mount Monadnock, rising nearly a thousand feet higher, and far grander in aspect. That night they saw a large fire burning on the distant peak. It lit the whole horizon and made Henry and his companion feel that they were a part of a greater community of mountains, and not so alone as they had imagined. The next day, before dawn, as if in communion, they made their own blaze.

This was in a time when the concept of small fires for cooking had not yet taken hold; Henry was always lighting immense fires to cook simple meals — fires so large, in fact, one might suspect that they served some additional purpose. Zoroastrians also kindled fires on peaks in honor of their god Almimar, the benign deity of goodness and light; and the spiritual symbolism of heights, the idea of gaining ground above the base earth, the aspiring toward light, was very much a part of nineteenth century transcendental thinking. It is not surprising that, seeing from Wachusett the greater heights of Monadnock, Henry would feel compelled to climb it too.

He first went up Monadnock two years after he had climbed Wachusett, and he made three subsequent trips there, spending eleven nights all told on the summit. The Indians of the region had a legend that the mountain contained rich veins of silver and gold, which would be discovered only after the human com-

munity was able to use the precious metals to their proper end —
the gold to honor the sun, the silver to honor the moon. Current
New Age theories hold that seven ley lines, or currents of energy
and power, cross at Monadnock, and in our time the region
around the mountain has become a center for people from a
variety of religious traditions. But Henry's writings about the
mountain deal more with the natural history of the area than
its spiritual overtones.

He did speak of the mysterious passing voices of the nighthawks as a fitting accompaniment for the thrumming, rocky
chords of the mountains — "strains from the music of Chaos,"
as he wrote — and he did seem to link the mountain with the
wilder high peaks of the world, Ararat and the Caucasus Mountains, where Prometheus was chained. But generally, in southern
New England, the landscaped world below and the rocky heights
above seemed comfortably balanced. Henry did not despair and
tremble on Monadnock as he had on the inhuman, chaotic
heights of Katahdin.

In 1844, the same year that he first scaled Monadnock, Thoreau went alone to western Massachusetts and climbed Mount
Greylock. This trip came at a low ebb in his life. He had recently
returned from a stay in New York, where he had failed to establish himself as a writer. The one outlet for his writings, *Dial*
magazine, had closed down. He had been working at his family's
pencil business that year, generally without much enthusiasm,
and that spring, in April, while on a boating trip up the Sudbury
River with a friend, he had accidentally started a forest fire that
burned over several hundred acres of precious wood lot in Concord. The trip to Greylock seems to have been in part a journey
of atonement, and an attempt to get some perspective on his
life.

He spent the night at a farmhouse in the area, and the next
day made his way straight up the mountain, passing directly
through the thick undergrowth rather than following any path.
The trees had a scraggly, infernal look, he wrote, "as if con-

tending with frost goblins." Forcing his way through them, he reached the summit of the mountain just as the sun was setting. He had time to observe the countryside before dark, and he made a small fire and collected some boards — part of an observatory that had been constructed on the summit. He did not have a tent with him, and the night was turning cold, so he built a shelter out of the boards, an oblong structure very like a coffin. He crawled inside and pulled some boards over his head to form a roof, which he held down with a heavy rock. Sheltered in this way from the cold wind, hard through his bed must have been, he reports that he slept well.

When he woke, he found himself in another world, as if he had died in the night and come alive again. Clouds had moved in and had settled over the valley and the lower peaks around him. He imagined that his coffinlike shelter was a boat, floating aloft above the clouds. The known world had disappeared, and as the light increased, the splendor of this higher country revealed itself.

It is perhaps difficult for us, in an age when flight above the cloud cover is an ordinary experience, to appreciate the awe he must have felt at finding himself above the clouds. Getting to a high spot above the common ground of the everyday world was an event in itself; rising above the very clouds of the sky must have been a transcendent experience even for the prosaic, and Henry was hardly prosaic.

He recorded the impression in his book *A Week on the Concord and Merrimack Rivers*

> All around beneath me was spread for a hundred miles on every side, as far as the eye could reach, an undulating country of clouds, answering in the varied swell of its surface to the terrestrial world it veiled. It was such a country as we might see in dreams, with all the delights of paradise. There were immense snowy pastures, apparently smooth-shaven and firm, and shady vales between the vaporous

mountains, and far in the horizon I could see where some
luxurious misty timber jutted into the prairie, and trace
the windings of a water course, some unimagined Amazon
or Orinoko, by the misty trees on its brink. . . .

The earth beneath had become such a flitting thing of
lights and shadows as the clouds had been before. It was
not merely veiled to me, but it has passed away like the
phantom of a shadow. . . . As I had climbed above storm
and cloud, so by successive days' journeys I might reach
the region of eternal day beyond the tapering shadow of
the earth.

At sunrise he found himself a dweller in the "dazzling halls
of Aurora"; saffron clouds drifted over the rosy fingers of dawn,
and he saw there the far-darting glances of the god of the sun.
He was renewed.

He descended Greylock later that morning and met a friend
that same day in Pittsfield. He was worn out by his experience
on the mountain. He was unshaven, seedily dressed, and dishev-
eled from sleeping in his clothes. But he had come to terms with
something. Astute readers of the account have pointed out that
he seems to have experienced a rebirth on Greylock, philosoph-
ically and perhaps spiritually. Within a year he would move to
Walden Pond, and during his two years there not only maintain
his journal and complete his book *A Week,* but also write the
book that made his reputation.

Henry made other ascents during his life. Two years later he
went up Katahdin. He climbed Monadnock again in 1852, then
again in 1858 and 1860. He climbed Kineo in Maine, the White
Mountains, and Fall Mountain in Vermont. True to form, he
compared these heights with the more famous peaks of the
known world, but it is certainly a pity that in his time, before
the opening up of Japan, he could have had no knowledge of
the greatest height of all in spiritual terms — Fujiyama. Henry's
Monadnock and Mount Fuji are linked by more than spiritual

overtones: they are now the two most commonly climbed mountains in the world.

My father's literary idol, Lafcadio Hearn, climbed Fuji and had an experience that was similar to Thoreau's vision on Greylock. Like Henry, he was ever alert to the symbolic overtones of mountains, and he was acutely aware of the religious significance that Fuji holds for the Japanese.

The summit of Fujiyama is the most sacred place in all of Japan. Arguably the most beautiful mountain in the world, Fuji is the very altar of the sun, the first spot in Japan to be touched at dawn. Shinto tradition holds that Fuji rose out of the earth in a single night. It is said that once, centuries ago, a shower of jewels fell from the heights, and that on certain occasions a misty, luminous maiden can be seen hovering over the crater. The peak is sacred to the Shinto: the deity Ko-no-hane-saku-hime dwells there, and a temple was constructed on the summit a thousand years ago to honor her. Buddhists also hold Fuji in awe. Its white peak represents the bud of the sacred lotus, and the eight cusps of the volcanic crater signify the eightfold path.

For more than a thousand years, pilgrims from all parts of Japan have ascended Fujiyama to watch the sun rise over the sea. Even in Thoreau's time, Fuji was a common pilgrimage site. It was the duty of all the reverent to climb it once in a lifetime, but since not everyone could afford to make the journey, pilgrimage societies were formed in small villages to send representatives to the holy mountain.

It is no wonder that Fuji is so revered. Rising nearly 12,500 feet above sea level, the mountain is visible from thirteen provinces in Japan, a distant white apparition, huge and domineering. Sometimes in spring and autumn, when the summit is still covered with snow, the snowless base takes on the color of the sky so that the great white peak floats free, apparently suspended in the blue upper air — a vast inverted fan hanging alone in the heavens. One does not live with indifference beneath such an eminence.

Lafcadio climbed Fuji at the end of August 1897. He traveled to the village of Gotemba, spent a sleepless night in one of the little pilgrim inns of the village, and began his ascent early the next morning, accompanied by several *goriki,* or Fuji guides.

Over the thousand years pilgrims have been ascending Fuji, certain traditions and traveler's aids have been established to assist them. Among these are the Fuji stations — wooden houses and huts, some dug into the mountain slopes, where pilgrims can rest, eat, and get supplies. There were ten of these stations between the base and the summit in Lafcadio's time, and they provided welcome relief for those who were not in good shape for the climb. Fuji pilgrims traditionally dress in white, carry long staves, and during poor weather cover themselves with straw mats and wide-brimmed hats. During the ascent, the staff is branded at each station with a *kenji* character indicating the place.

Lafcadio was perhaps not in the best shape for an ascent of Fuji. Never in perfect health — among other things he suffered from poor eyesight all his life — he began, as did many pilgrims, on horseback, riding to station two and a half, where he dismounted and began walking through the soft ashes and cinders that characterize the upper slopes of Fuji. It was cloudy and foggy, as it often is on Fuji, but periodically the fog would pull back and reveal the black slope of the mountain looming ahead of his little party. Slowly, station by station, zigzagging all the way, the group rose. The air turned cold. They reached a great stretch of snow, forced their way through the wind, and by 4:30 that afternoon, having attained the eighth station at 10,600 feet, they decided to rest for the night.

Lafcadio was completely exhausted. Even though it was August, the night was bitterly cold. The climbers wrapped themselves in thick blue robes, built a fire, lit the lamps for the night, and prepared to sleep. Cold and tired though he was, Lafcadio could not tear himself away from the vision beyond him. Night was falling, the stars were flickering in a blue-black sky, and the world below had disappeared.

Traditionally the cloud world below Fuji is called the Sea of Cotton, but as he looked out over this impossible landscape, the long swells of the cotton balls settled, and a great white seemingly self-illuminated flood of clouds spread out below him as far as he could see. Lafcadio had another image.

"It is a Sea of Milk," he wrote in his account of the ascent. "The Cosmic Sea of ancient Indian legend — and always self-luminous as with ghostly quickenings."

That night he listened attentively to the folk tales of Fuji shared by the *goriki* in the warm hut. Just before he went to sleep he was warned not to go outdoors alone, although the *goriki* would not tell him exactly why. He woke at four in the morning and, in spite of the warning, stepped out onto the slopes. Over the Sea of Milk the moon was dying; the wind was filled with ice, and above him the dark slope rose ominously, stretching up into the black nothingness of the sky. The *goriki* were out after him in a second and pulled him back in. Fuji slopes are alive with spirits at night, they said. Once, centuries before, the Luminous Maiden had lured an emperor to the crater, and he was never seen again. There is a little shrine on the summit to mark the point of his disappearance. Sand that rolls down the slopes of Fuji by day, loosened by the feet of pilgrims, rolls back up again at night, when no one is watching. Fascinated though he was with the macabre and the supernatural, Lafcadio went inside.

The next morning they made the summit. Lafcadio was horrified by the broken volcanic landscape, the scarlike ridges, the vast jagged walls, the hideous overhanging black cusps. But the view beyond was wreathed in clouds, a phantasmagoric landscape. The Sea of Milk had billowed up again, great rents had opened, and the yellow glare of the wind-blown fire of the sun ran along the eastern horizon where a ragged edge of purple cloud was infused with a red glow like that of burning charcoal. All around him he could hear the rhythmic clapping of the Shinto pilgrims as they prayed to the sun. But they were denied the sunrise. The clouds rolled back in, the east was obscured, and, still fatigued, Lafcadio descended into the warmer foothills.

He incorporated his experience on Fuji into a retelling of a Japanese legend. In the story a seeker of knowledge ascends a steep mountain, guided by the bodhisattva. The climb is not easy. They rise above the cosmic Sea of Milk, pass hideous, ghostly outcroppings, very like the slopes of Fuji, and finally, near the summit, come to the realization that the mountain consists entirely of human skulls. Each one, the bodhisattva explains, belongs to the pilgrim himself, the accumulation of all his millions of past lives.

My father climbed Mount Fuji on August 6, 1916. He too left from Gotemba after a sleepless night and ascended part of the way on horseback, although he and his companion, a man named Green, dismounted sooner than Lafcadio and began walking. They had been issued at the inn the traditional Fuji accoutrements — the four pairs of sandals, the warm underwear, and the long staffs. For a while that day my father even wore the straw pilgrim mat but found it cumbersome and discarded it. Shortly before they dismounted, while they were still in the foothills, they came across a regiment of soldiers who had set up field artillery and were pointlessly lobbing shells into a distant green hillside. The war machine of Japan, which would come to an end at Hiroshima on that very date twenty-nine years in the future, was already in the process of being built. The irony of soldiers on the slopes of a sacred mountain was not lost on my father.

He and Green moved through deciduous woods, ascended into the pines, and finally broke out into the loose cinders of the open slopes. The climbing became more difficult as the grade increased; the weather turned cold, and the traditional clouds of Fuji enveloped them, although after another hour or so, the sky cleared for a spell. Periodically on the upper slopes they would pass small groups of pilgrims, straw mats tied to their backs. They overtook one such group shortly after they cleared the cloud cover. They were wearing bells, clad in the traditional white of Fuji pilgrims, and as my father and Green climbed onward, they could hear behind them the eerie clanging of the bells below the clouds, and strange, intertwining chanting floating up from the nothingness below them. Ahead they could see the great shining peak, the sun above it, each rock throwing a brilliantly clear shadow. They pushed on, fatigued but determined.

By the time they reached station number eight, where Lafcadio had spent the night, it was 6:30 P.M. They were nearly exhausted, but after a bowl of soup and eggs, they climbed higher. Below them, even in the pale light of dusk, they could see now the great billowing skyscape of clouds, a long snow field of white tinged here and there in the deeper crevices with a shadowed blue. The immense dark outline of Fuji itself fell across the clouds. They reached the summit just before nine o'clock, utterly exhausted.

At a station on the summit, they spent the night, lying on the hard floor, packed in with the other Fuji pilgrims, while an oil lamp swung above them and the charcoal braziers gave off a warm, smoky light. In spite of his fatigue my father could not sleep. The stone hut was crowded, and pilgrims were moving about all night. The high winds howled. The lamp smoked over his head, and he spent the night waiting for dawn. At some point he became aware that more pilgrims were stirring, and he realized that he and Green had not been called for the rising of the sun as they had requested, which must have meant that the clouds had rolled in again. He turned over, warm in his comforter, and as the gray light suffused the interior, he watched the little groups of returning pilgrims. Those who had been outside waiting for the sun came back in, their clothes drenched.

They were shivering and soaked, but even though they had not witnessed the rising of their god above the blue sea, they were in good spirits. They undressed for bed, ate their steaming bowls of rice, and fell asleep around him.

Green and my father went down later that morning, slipping and glissading all the way. Behind them, the sky now clear, floated the great peak, silent and overbearing. Even after their descent it floated there above them, first in actuality, and then later in my father's imagination. The ascent of Fuji was one of the most memorable experiences of his life; thirty years later he was still telling stories about it.

My father brought home from the East the staff he had used to climb Fujiyama. He carried it with him through his various moves, and took it north when he finally settled outside New York City, where I was born. I remember it well from my childhood; it has a certain smell or aura about it. When I moved into my cottage and began reading my father's journals of China and Japan, I got the staff from my brother Hugh. It was splintered and rough, but the black Japanese characters were still clearly visible, and it still had the ability to summon in me images of my father's experiences on Fuji. It is one of the many artifacts from the East that I either remember vividly or continue to live with: the statue of the man with the headlike bowl, the books of Lafcadio Hearn, a beautiful cloisonné opium pipe, and of course the stories — night after night of stories.

Sometimes in the cottage, just before I fell asleep, all these artifacts and events would become confused in my mind. The staff, the bowl, my father's experiences in the East would coexist with the secret places of the ridge, the hemlock grove, the Pawtucket burial places, the mist-shrouded hollows, and the dark, interior spaces of the woods. Time and space would dissolve; the ridge would become the world.

My father left the Orient on July 11, 1918. The United States had entered the war, and he had decided to leave his teaching post and join the army. His last view of the East was of Yokohama harbor, where the ship had stopped to take on coal and passengers. He recorded the event in his journal:

As I write, the ship resounds with the activities which precede departure. All morning the loading of boxes and of coal has been hectic and now, with the time of leaving only three quarters of an hour away, the derrick is still feverishly working, and the air is filled with coal dust. We are so laden that the waterline has risen perceptibly. This should at least prevent rolling in heavy weather.

New passengers have been coming on board all morning, and tiffin was a gala event with many Japanese in their flowery gowns or in uniform and gold lace. And now final farewells are being said. My time in the East is short.

The excitement gradually increased as the scheduled time of leaving drew near. The last cargo to come aboard was a great pile of mail bags which were swung up the cranes in their bags of netting. Then the whistle sounded and the gongs beat. Those who had come on board to say goodbye began hurriedly to leave over the high gangplank, adding the gay colors of Japanese clothing and the white of the foreigners to the ugly gray of the wharf. A final whistle as the ship's bell struck six, and the straining coolies pushed away the gangplank and began to cast off the hawsers.

There is an emotional thrill in all leave taking, and it is particularly keen when a big ship puts off. In our case too we were going home — most of us after years in the Orient. And when one goes home in wartime, it is to unknown conditions and an unknown future.

The crowd on the ship cracked jokes and made light of it, as people always do when they really feel a thrill. They broke jokingly into "Over There" as we warped away from the dock, but they really meant it: "The Yanks are coming, the Yanks are coming; and we won't be back until its over

over there." There was cheering on the dock and the usual waving of hats and handkerchiefs.

A puffing tug pulled our bow around until we headed out between the red and white lighthouses which mark the breakwater of Yokohama harbor. And we steamed slowly out and into the blue-green water and whitecaps of the Pacific. It had been 96 degrees in the shade in Yokohama; out in the harbor there was a splendid cool breeze. The skyline was piled up with fleecy white clouds and so we could not see Fuji to say goodbye. We were sorry for that, for there is a superstition that unless one can say goodbye to Fuji as he leaves Yokohama harbor, he is not coming back to the East.

14 Living at
the End of Time

 ONCE, YEARS AGO, I spent some time hiking in
the Cévennes Mountains in southern France. One day I came
to a ravine with a stream running through it. I had been walking
all day, and the brook and the ferny cliff face beside it were
wonderfully inviting, so I took off my shoes, cooled my feet in
the waters, and then lay back on the mossy bank to rest. It was
a dry, hot Provençal summer day, the type of day that brings
out the resinous odors of the local herbs and sets the cicadas
calling. I could hear their brittle whispers in the groves and dry
hillsides beyond the ravine. By the stream the air was cooler and
smelled of moisture and rank plants, and I lay there, listening
to the ripple of the water over the riffles and the incessant dry
rattle of the cicadas. I think I fell asleep for a minute or two,
and in this half-state I sensed that something had come into the
ravine. I opened my eyes and saw, or dreamed I saw, a hideous
bearded face with loose lips, yellowed teeth, and a curving sweep
of ringed horns curling beside its head. I leaped up. But there
was only the tripping of the stream, the overpowering, shushing
call of the insects. Then I heard a scrambling and the clatter of
dry stones on the hill behind me. I was alone again.

The area I was hiking through was rich in ruins. Everywhere
I went I would come across the remnants of various cultures
that had existed in that part of the world for more than two

thousand years — medieval Christian churches, Roman walls, towers, and aqueducts. In the dry valleys and hills there was an aura of the classic pastoral of goatherds and shepherds. In fact what I had probably seen — if indeed I was awake — was a goat. But I couldn't shake the strong impression that Pan or some other deity, some resident spirit of the ravine, had been watching me. I went back into the brush on the hillside and looked for goat signs — droppings or tracks or nipped-off branches. There were none.

I thought about that event for years. It seemed to say something about the nature of a landscape, the nature or sense of a place. I used to walk around the woods in North America with a feeling that something was missing, that somehow the land was incomplete or lonely. The event in the Cévennes identified the thing that was missing from the American landscape — namely the human element, the feeling of a land that had been lived in and worshipped by a people. During the time that I lived on the ridge, I came to realize my mistake. I had been expecting the wrong thing.

If indeed the American land has a spirit, if there is, as cultures throughout history have believed, some god overseeing the forests and hills, then here in North America it must be one of the fifteen-thousand-year-old deities of the people who inhabited the continent for the better part of its human history. It must be the T'chi Manitou, the creative force of the Algonquian people. It is Hobomacho, Menobohzo, and all the other spirits, giants, wood dwarfs, and monsters of the American Indian pantheon. Time and technology have not yet managed to obliterate them.

I had further evidence of this that spring. With the onset of warmer weather, almost every day I would walk back to the hemlock grove, sometimes just to visit the place, sometimes to use it as a starting point for a longer walk on the ridge. For me the grove was like one of those little processional chapels where penitents would stop during festivals and ceremonial parades.

Nothing ever happened there. The trees were generally empty of bird life, and there were no flowers or shrubs growing on the darkened forest floor; but the place drew me in nonetheless.

One morning toward the end of May, while I was sitting in the grove, I heard a mysterious bird singing in the high branches, a bright yellow form whose markings I could not see clearly. I do not like hearing songs I cannot recognize, and I spent a long time outside the grove with binoculars trying to get a better view. Finally the bird left the cover of the branches and flew down the west slope of the ridge, through the oak trees, still singing. I followed after it, lost it, followed it some more, and then lost it completely; but all across the hillside, from a thousand trees and shrubs, I could hear the great rolling dawn chorus of other birds.

This particular bird had led me to a small terrace of pines, an area I did not recognize, but since it was still early and the day was fine, I continued down the slope with no particular destination in mind. I crossed a stone wall and walked downhill, through a tangle of brush, thinking that I should come in due course to the old wagon road that led to the lake where Megan Lewis and Emil and Minna lived. The road wasn't there. Neither was the oak tree that stood near it, towering above the other, lesser trees of the ridge. I was lost again.

I could not say how much of my habit of getting lost in the woods on the ridge was intentional. Elsewhere in the world I seem to have an unerring sense of direction, but here the landmarks moved. The sun changed course; the walls and old roads disappeared. On that day I simply wandered deeper into the maze, forced my way through a tangle of brush, and then broke out into a flat ground of white pine where the floor of the woods was clear of undergrowth and spread over with yellowish fallen needles. I lay down on the soft ground and stared up at the network of branches, listening to the birds sing. There were robins and buntings and thrushes, and I could hear close by the eerie descending song of the veery. Warblers were singing from the oaks behind me; a blue jay screamed. Somewhere to the south a flock of crows began to call, and then, suddenly, I heard the bird I had followed earlier. I did not move this time. I won't say I had lost interest. But the effort of getting up from the soft bed of pine to follow its song through the snagging tangle of vegetation beyond the pines seemed too much work for so fine a spring morning. The bird passed overhead, calling incessantly, a repeated series of chips. It stopped singing for a minute. I closed my eyes, opened them, and there it was in front of me. It was a Canada warbler, a bird I had not seen or heard since I lived in southern Connecticut some twenty years earlier. The sight of it brought on a surge of memories of walks in spring woodlands. I got up to follow.

The warbler moved out of the pines into some undergrowth, and then, still singing, flew into the trees again. I tried to catch up but got tangled in brush and decided to quit. It was getting hot now, and the air was very still. Just beyond the undergrowth, somewhere high among the leaves, the Canada warbler continued to sing, as if daring me to find it, but I had a sense suddenly that I should not move. The warbler sounded out; a blue jay called, and far off the barking of crows continued. I waited. A vast stillness descended over the ridge like a blanket. I felt like a hunter on the verge of a kill, spear drawn back, muscles tightening for the cast. Someone or something was nearby.

In the midst of the silence the Canada warbler called out again, and then in front of me, not ten yards away, I saw a beautiful red fox looking at me, its tail curled around its forelegs. As soon as our eyes met, it disappeared without a sound. I hardly had time to realize it had been there; it simply spun and fled up the ridge. I stepped out of the tangle and unexpectedly found myself on the old wagon road, not far from the Pawtucket burial ground. The fox was standing in the road, looking back over its shoulder. But as soon as it saw me, it streaked up the hill toward the boulders where the Indians were supposedly buried. I could see the rocks in front of me, gray-green, rounded shapes among the trees, standing like the broken columns of a ruined temple, and there among them I counted five white-tailed deer, brown fur against the green moss, their ears turned toward me, their eyes large and curious and serene.

I waited. They waited. I stepped forward. They twitched their ears. I took another step, and they spun on their hooves and dashed full tilt up the hill, tails flashing white, hoofbeats thumping the ground. In midflight one of them stopped and turned to face me. It stood alone, head held high, ears pointed forward. Then slowly, as I watched unmoving, it lifted its right leg elegantly, and with all the grace of some proud flamenco dancer, stamped its hoof hard against the ground. It walked forward a few paces, head still high, and repeated the stamp, slower this time, and with more grace. We faced each other in this manner for a full two minutes, and in the space of that time a single name came into my head — T'chi Manitou. This was more than a thought; it seemed that the words actually rang out among the trees, and in fact had the deer not barked sharply, stamped again, and then followed the others up the hill, I would have said that it spoke the name. But then perhaps I had been thinking too much about Doctor John's story of the tiger in India. I went in among the boulders and sat down for a while, listening to the stillness and the periodic cries of the blue jays. There was a rustle of wind, and then a deeper quiet descended on the ridge. The sense of a haunted land was everywhere.

The fireflies hatched early in the meadow that June. I saw the first one just after dusk on the eighteenth, a bright spark against the black wall of the trees. It was at first a mere glow, a reflection of dew I thought, until I saw it rise above the grass, flashing, and spirit off to the east. Several others appeared that night, and after two or three days they were everywhere, filling the meadow with light. Henry saw fireflies on the sixteenth of June in 1852 on an evening walk. There was heat lightning that evening on the horizon, and somewhere in the village someone was playing a flute. Beyond on the river, a mile distant, he could hear the rolling chorus of the bullfrogs. The night was hot, the air close, and in the meadows around him the bright flashes of the fireflies were sparkling. They were like fallen stars, and in their light he envisioned a union of sky and earth, each showing its light "for love," as he wrote.

In 1852 he had been gone from his cabin at Walden Pond for five years. He left, he said, for the same reason that he went there, because he had other lives to lead. Perhaps he realized that staying on would have dulled the experience. He continued to explore the natural world of Concord after he moved out, but he did not have that many years left.

In spite of his outdoor, elemental life, Henry was not entirely healthy. His lungs had probably been weakened by his work in his father's dusty pencil factory. Late in 1860 Henry was visited by his friend Bronson Alcott, who was suffering at the time from a bad cold. Henry caught the cold and it worsened into bronchitis, as his colds often did. He spent the winter housebound and weakened. He was still weak in the spring, and his doctor suggested that he go to a better climate, so Henry went off to — of all places — Minnesota. He spent two months there, studying the natural history of the region and, among other things, attending an Indian dance and ceremony. He was back in Concord by July, uncured, and that fall he was still in poor health. The problem by this time was not bronchitis but tuberculosis.

Henry had developed a more scientific interest in the natural world in his later years; he was studying and classifying trees and their history, and that winter, sick as he was, his work continued unabated. But it was not a good winter. The journal, the real work of his short life, ended in November with relatively light entries about the behavior of kittens and a storm.

January was cold that year, with high winds. An old man who was a friend of Henry's and a source of much of the folklore of the town, died. Henry developed pleurisy and was confined to his bed. By the end of winter it was clear that he was dying.

His was not a quick death. He was so weak he could speak only in whispers; the ominous flush of tuberculosis tinted his cheeks. He was living at home at this time with his mother and his last living sister, Sophia, and he insisted on having his bed moved downstairs to the living room so he could enjoy the life of the household till the end. In spite of his weakness, he continued to work, and, as everyone who visited him at this period remarked, his spirits were good — high almost, some said. His former jailer, Sam Staples, commented that he never saw a man die in such pleasure and peace. Henry was on the brink of the next world, and true to form, he seemed curious to enter it; he was ever the explorer. He continued to be attached to the world of the living, however. A friend visiting him, a man who was not afraid to speak directly, asked whether he might perhaps be able to see the "other side of the dark river." "One world at a time," Henry answered. Another visitor asked him if he had finally made his peace with God. "I was not aware," said Henry, "that we have ever quarreled." This was not a man trembling in the face of dissolution.

Early on the morning of May 6, 1862, he and his sister were reading sections of the manuscript of *A Week on the Concord and Merrimack Rivers*. It was a fitting project for a man whose life had, in some ways, been inspired and shaped by his relationship with his brother and their early years together. He was obviously preoccupied by events of that period of his life. Even on his deathbed, when Ellen Sewall's name came up Henry said, "I have always loved her."

Henry was too weak by this time to hold the manuscript, to read or make corrections, so Sophia would read aloud to him. She had come to the last chapter, the point at which Henry and his brother are approaching the mouth of the Nashua River, where it flows into the Merrimack. The narrative digresses at this point.

> There is a pleasant tract on the bank of the Concord, called Conantum, which I have in my mind, — the old deserted farmhouse. The desolate pasture with its bleak cliff, the open wood, the river-reach, the green meadow in the midst, and the moss-grown wild-apple orchard, — places where one may have many thoughts and not decide anything. It is a scene which I can not only remember, as I might a vision, but when I will can bodily revisit.

She read on. Henry was still, his breathing ever more shallow.

"There is something even in the lapse of time by which time recovers itself," she read.

It was a cool and breezy day on the Merrimack. The two brothers sat muffled in their cloaks while the river and the wind carried them along. They passed farms and homesteads where women and children stood on the bank, staring at them until they had swept out of sight.

The river rippled and bounded.

"We glided past the mouth of the Nashua, and not long after, of Salmon Brook, without more pause than the wind."

Sophia stopped reading. The two brothers were carried ever downstream, and downwind to Concord, a wild, easy ride. Henry knew the narrative by heart. "Now comes good sailing," he said.

After that he said something else. Sophia could not catch the full sentence, but Henry was somewhere back in Maine, somewhere in wilderness.

"Moose," he whispered. "Indian."

It was still early morning. Outside, spring was reawakening. The black and white warblers had returned, the flickers were whinnying from the distant wood lots, the smell of fresh soil filled the air, and the new leaves of the oaks and the maples made a lace work of the morning sky. Inside, the chronicler of such events was dead.

*

I saw Kenny Olsen that month. He was waiting in line in the
post office. Slouched over, dressed in corduroy and flannel, he
looked more like a local electrician than the president of a multinational corporation. He would be getting ready, I thought,
for his annual trip to Maine.

Although he could afford yachts and exotic vacations, Uncle
Kenny prefers to go canoeing in the North Woods of Maine, a
region beloved by Henry Thoreau. There, for a week or two,
while all around the world his computers continue their work,
he roughs it in the wilderness, sleeping on the ground, paddling
through placid lakes, dashing through the rapids of white-water
rivers, and portaging through musky swamps and bogs. Uncle
Kenny is a man of simple tastes; he prefers a low profile, keeps
his horizons in sight, and, just to remind himself of his summer
trips, keeps in his living room in Lincoln, Massachusetts, a stuffed
beaver, a memory of the North Country.

When I saw him there in the post office, it occurred to me to
go up and introduce myself. I would tell him about my interest
in his business, tell him about my "conversion" on the plane trip
back from Puerto Rico. I might even tell him about my quest to
get inside his plant. I glanced at Uncle Kenny — possibly I fixed
his eye, since he looked up and nodded seriously — but in the
end I simply returned his nod and moved out the door. I watched
him through the plate glass window of the post office as he slowly
and obediently shuffled forward to the counter. I could see him
almost apologetically negotiating with the clerk as he posted his
small, carefully wrapped package.

None of this modesty keeps Kenny from building large plants,
of course — that is an essential part of his business — and that
spring, as promised, work began on the second wing of the great
city on the hill, an exact replica of the first wing. When completed
the structure would double the number of employees working
at that facility, and would, in a single sweep, substantially increase
the size of the daytime population of the town.

Late in May I happened to see my friend in the cowboy hat

getting into his Saab in the Digital parking lot. I stopped to ask him what progress he was making on my request to visit the plant. He had actually returned my phone calls, and we had been chatting on and off for a number of weeks. We talked some more in the parking lot and then went across the street for a drink.

We sat at an outdoor café that had opened recently, one of many new businesses that had sprung up because of the presence of the Digital employees. I liked the café. From the terrace I could not see the monster plant. What was left of the pear orchard was just across the street, and just beyond, a great copper beech tree obscured — for the most part — a new gas station that had been built off the town common to serve the new highway. We sat there watching the sun set over the pear orchard while the computer man told me about innovations in networking and superconductivity and what all this would mean for the future. I became lost early on in his speech. I was thinking of the big barn that used to stand beyond the orchard. It would have made an excellent frame for the dying sun. Somewhere in the midst of his explanation of networks I heard him say that I could see this system when I visited the plant.

"You mean it's okay to come?" I asked.

"Yes, I just said that. I think it's okay. You're clearly not an industrial spy."

"Ah, but I am," I answered truthfully. "Of the worst sort."

"So am I," he said. "Fifth Column."

The sun dipped below the ridge of high ground — the same ridge on which my little cottage sat. We set up a day and a time for my visit; I paid for the drinks and we parted.

June tenth of that year was a day so rare, so precious, that to lose even a minute of it by going indoors seemed sinful. Out in my garden a few days earlier the yellow day lilies had come into bloom; the indigo bunting had returned, and everywhere the world was lush and green. I was up very early that morning, and I went down to scythe the meadow and listen to the rolling dawn chorus. There was not a single cloud; the sky had assumed a deep aquamarine color, a translucence that caused the grasses, trees, and rocks to stand out in brilliant detail. The air was so clear that perception of distance was diminished; everything was wet and close and sharp. I scythed for a while and then walked around the meadow and the garden looking at the little foaming clusters of spittle bugs, sniffing the morning air, and searching for new seedlings. The sun gained; the shadows shortened and darkened; the air began to dry; and out on the main road, the tidal flow of commuting traffic began to swell. In the distance, in the clear air, I could hear the dull roar of its passage.

I began to regret that I had agreed to meet my new acquaintance at the Digital plant at four that afternoon. Working in the knee-high grasses, swinging the scythe, I remembered asking a friend of mine who has a good job at Digital what he feels in the parking lot on a lovely spring morning, just before entering into the closed world of computers.

"Anxiety," he answered without deliberation.

I scythed some more. The first cutting of the year is always the best. The grass is water-filled and tender and clips off neatly with the slightest stroke. Row by row I proceeded, cutting up from the lower end of the meadow toward the garden and the western wall. The day was invigorating, and some flow or spirit in the air kept me working. The indigo buntings spilled out their long, bubbling music; the scent of fresh grass rose in almost visible lines, shimmering; and as I cut, little sprays of retreating insects flew up ahead of me.

Megan Lewis would be outdoors today. I had seen her a week or so earlier in a garden center in the nearby town of Lexington. She was making pronouncements on the stock, and she was clearly back in form. She seemed to have settled into a comfortable existence as a widow-gardener.

"Ever so boring, don't you think? They never seem to be able to import anything that is in any way interesting into these nurseries. You have to send away to the catalogues, or grow it your-self, which takes years."

"You have time," I said.

"In fact I don't. I turned seventy this winter, I think you should know. But I'm planting trees anyway. It's the least one can do."

The ridge and its people had all managed to adjust in one way or another. About a month before Higgins had showed up at my cottage and begun pacing around my terrace; after a while he told me, gravely, that for some time he and Jane had been in counseling together.

"Oh no," I said. "Problems?"

"No. We're getting married. The therapist said it's okay."

Emil and Minna were getting by. With their nest emptied, they had become even more dedicated to their self-sufficient way of life. They seemed to have adjusted to the presence of the Digital plant. Once I saw Minna standing on the town common staring at the building.

"Quite a change, isn't it?" I said.

"So quickly you get used to it," she answered sadly.

Not long after seven o'clock an executive helicopter flew over. It had probably taken off from southern New Hampshire, where a cluster of computer companies, including the ever-present Digital, had built new plants, and it was no doubt headed for another cluster somewhere along Route 128, near Boston. The economy was changing around here. Henry Thoreau, passing through this area in June, would have seen gangs of scythers moving slowly across the hay fields, whole teams of men and boys silently swinging in the early light of the morning while the dew was still heavy on the hay.

I rested for a while in the garden, drank some cold water, listened to the birds, and then went back to work. I had cut a large section already, more than I usually do in a morning, and since I was making good time and had no other responsibilities that day — except my Digital appointment — I decided to cut over the whole meadow. I went back and began at the south wall. A chestnut-sided warbler was singing madly in the oak tree behind me. I moved down the row, cutting evenly, pacing myself and listening to the fine, watery swish of the blade. A slow-moving garter snake wriggled up a bundle of fallen stems and halted for a second or two, eyeing me and flicking its tongue. I moved and it disappeared, the exquisite stripes and dots merging with the greens of the meadow.

Where is Prince Rudolph today, I wondered? It was the type of day he loved, the kind of clear, dry weather that put him on the road to someplace other than where he happened to be. I had seen him a week or so earlier on a similarly brilliant day, striding west on Route 2, his battered suitcase in hand and his ever-present winter coat thrown over his right shoulder. There was a bounce in his walk that suggested he might be in a better mood than he generally was, and I pulled over to ask if he wanted a ride.

"No thanks," he said with unusual friendliness. "I'm walking."

Then he seemed to recognize me. "Me and a buddy are going to get one of them trailers and head west. We're going to Tucson. They got a good park there by the rail line. What do I care? Know what I mean? I've had it with winters up here anyway. This one nearly took me down."

"Well, good luck."

"Yeah," he said. "Good luck." He snorted, tossed his head cynically and walked away.

About eight-thirty, the dull roar of the commuter traffic quieted and then ceased altogether. The sun warmed, climbed above the oaks on the lower fields, and then began to edge across the meadow. On the other side of the valley, in the great plant, the workers would be reading their electronic mail, punching up numbers on the screens, sending memos and jokes to one another across regions and continents. The light in their cubicles would be uniform, a white, unshadowed fluorescence.

My friend Susan, who had worked at Digital for five years

before quitting to spend more time with her daughter, used to say that sometimes when she was working at her terminal she would become so consumed by the lighted screen, the quick flashes of numerals and words, that she would lose track of time and forget to eat. One day she forgot to leave work on time to pick up her daughter at day care. When this happened a second time she arranged for a vacation. She rented a cabin on a hill in New Hampshire and spent two weeks trying to do nothing. She was edgy during the first week, but by the weekend she had become comfortable in the place. By the end of the second week, while she was out picking blueberries, it struck her that she could go on in this manner for a long time, picking blueberries with her daughter and feeling the heat of the sun on her back. She gave notice when she returned.

I stopped scything again halfway up the meadow and sat down in the shade of the hickory grove.

With the end of June approaching, and the upcoming anniversary of a year in the cottage, I had been spending more and more time thinking about what to do.

The idea of the cottage had begun as a temporary solution to a housing problem. But even before I began building, I knew that it was more than that. Quite apart from a commitment to my children, the decision to build was the result of an attachment to a place. This ridge, with its mysterious hollows, its hemlocks and hickory groves, was not especially remarkable, but for me the land provided a quiet center in the midst of a noisy world. And anyway, as Sanferd said, a place is what you make of it, not what it really is.

Yet there were certain economic realities about the region. The ridge was located at one of the technological crossroads of America, and the elements of the land that I had come to appreciate — the forest, the historical landscape — were probably doomed. I had been thinking recently about that part of the ridge that twentieth-century legal documents tell me I "own." I had placed my cottage on what is known in the trade as a build-

able lot, which meant that if I ever sold the land and moved
away, someone could come along and put up a house in "my"
meadow. Given the current architectural tastes of the developers
and contractors in the area, I had to assume that whatever appeared in the meadow would detract from the existing landscape. The alternative, of course, would be to beat them at their
own game and put up a house of my own — a proper one, in
the style of Andrew Jackson Downing, something that would suit
the nature of the ridge.

I doused myself with water and went back to the meadow to
continue mowing. In the clear, hot light of late morning the
woods beyond the stone walls had darkened to black, and the
air over the field was nearly white. The indigo buntings were
singing madly, the garden flowers were coming into bloom, and
there was nothing in view to indicate that this was the bitter end
of the twentieth century and we could all be living at the end of
time.

By noon the Digital workers would be streaming out of their
plant and walking down the roads of the community. Flowers
and strawberries and asparagus had been set out in the farm
stands along with what was left of the rural roads beyond the
plant, and whenever the weather was nice, the workers would
pick up bouquets and fruit or vegetables and after lunch walk
back with this locally grown produce to work at their terminals.
It seemed that a fairly rational balance had been achieved in this
spot. The fields and the orchards were still functioning, and
relatively clean, nonpolluting industries had been fitted in
among the natural areas and the housing. Even the wildlife
seemed to be holding its own. Earlier that month I had seen an
otter on Beaver Brook, not two hundred yards from a small
computer company.

I began cutting down another row, consumed now by the slow
rhythm of the scythe. In that single pass, three leopard frogs
dashed out from the cover of the grass and with grand, arching

leaps fled before the whispering blade. I thought of Levin in
Anna Karenina scything with his peasants in the meadows of
Russia, one of the great scything portraits of history. I thought
of my ninety-four-year-old friend Captain Bill Vinal — long
since dead now — who had told me stories of cutting salt hay
on the marshes of the North River in southeastern Massachusetts. In his youth in the 1890s he and his father and a gang of
boys would rise early in the morning, take the hay wagon to the
river marshes, and spend the day scything, drinking switchel —
the traditional beverage of scythers — and eating cucumbers
with bread and butter. There was always competition among
them to carry the heavier end of the hay load, which they would
transport to the wagon by ramming two long beams under the
haystack. Young Bill once asked his father if he could possibly
carry the heavy end. The old man fixed his eye. "You will carry
the heavy end soon enough," he said.

Perhaps I should be grateful to Uncle Kenny's city on the hill.
Where would we be without computers and electronics? What
would our culture be like without television, without video cas-
sette recorders or televised sporting events, which, on a brilliant
summer or autumn afternoon, when the sky is almost too blue
to bear, hold millions indoors? I should be grateful. Without
television they might all swarm over the landscape into the woods
and the meadows, littering and shooting birds and crowding
useless poets from their reveries.

Ah, Henry, thou should'st be living at this hour, New England
hath need of thee.

By the time the shadows began to lengthen in the meadow, I
had mowed up to the garden. It was time to meet my friend at
Digital. I hung the scythe in the shed, poured some cold water
into a basin on the front porch of my cottage, and washed up
in the open air. I changed into some clean clothes and checked
myself in a mirror I had hung on the back wall. It seemed to
me that I looked very brown from the sun. I would probably be

the only one at the plant that day who lived in such a primitive manner. But then I once knew a computer analyst who worked for a bank. He had a lot of money, but by choice he lived in the back of his car. By day he would appear in the bank in respectable clothing. By night he reverted to his gypsy car camp. We all have secret lives of one sort or another.

The day had been a fitting prelude to my visit. A wilder man than myself, a more committed naturalist such as Henry Thoreau, would never have mowed the grass in that meadow; he would have let the land take its natural course and grow back to forest. On the larger scale of history, the scythe is really only a few steps away from the computer, and in fact not that far removed from the bomb.

I parked my car in the visitors' lot at LKP 595 and walked up toward the front doors, passing along the way the dark wood of white pines which Uncle Kenny had left standing. For some reason I was reminded of Dante in the dark woods on the outskirts of hell. But in fact I was about to ascend into my long-sought-for city on the hill and meet my computer-age Virgil in his cowboy clothes.

The lobby was the scene of a great deal of activity. A conference was under way, and men from various alien computer companies were milling about, introducing themselves and exchanging cards. One poor man, an Indian, was lost and had arrived at the wrong Digital plant. I waited at the desk while the receptionist explained to him how to get to the other plant some twenty miles down the highway. I stepped to the counter after he left, explained my mission as instructed by my friend, and then signed my name and the date in the great Book of Names. A column requesting "Affiliation" threw me for a few seconds. It was a good question.

The nice receptionist instructed me to take a seat and explained that Virgil would be down soon. Outside, beyond the sealed plate glass windows, which because of the climate-controlled environment of the plant were designed to discourage the entry of even the slightest draft of fresh air, the languid summer afternoon was winding slowly toward a generous evening. I could see the wind stirring the trees and grass, but it was like watching a silent film of nature — no smells, no sounds, no feel of air and sun. Inside, a vaguely institutional sense of a hospital dominated. There were concrete walls, cold, uninviting couches, racks of literature advertising Digital innovations, and, spread over low tables, computer magazines. I tried to read one of them. They were written in English, but the meaning was unfathomable to me.

My friend did not appear. I waited. I looked out the window a while longer, regretting the flight of a fine afternoon. I watched a group of men behind a glass wall finishing up a conference. They were standing around in their shirtsleeves, shaking hands and sorting through papers. Some looked like Mexican bandits, with wide, turned-down mustaches; some looked like stereotypical technocrats, with their shirt-pocket pen protectors; and some appeared to be ordinary businessmen in three-piece suits.

I poked around some more, found an application for employment at Digital, and, having nothing better to do, filled it out. No one was paying any attention to me. The guards were relaxed, there were crowds of people, and I began to wander beyond my appointed range. I passed through some glass doors and came to a long hallway lined with blank walls. I turned around and saw, on my left, another large, glassed-in room. There, inside, I saw row on row of computers, clicking away unattended, like a private brain for the building. I stood watching in awe, feeling somewhat dizzied by the magnitude of the room, the seemingly random, independent energy of the computers. Someone opened a door at the other end of the hall, and I fled back into the lobby, disoriented.

The conference men emerged just then and surrounded me. They were now in the highest of spirits, and to escape them I crossed the lobby, checked to see whether Virgil had appeared, and then, still disoriented, started down another hall on the north side of the building. There was a signboard on the wall, listing, I thought, the names of the people who worked in the various offices, and in an effort to locate Virgil I began reading through them. The names sounded very familiar to me, very New England, and then suddenly I thought I was losing my mind. There, emblazoned in bright letters, working, as the sign explained, on the second floor, was Henry David Thoreau.

I looked again, unbelieving. "Henry David Thoreau," it read, "Second Floor."

I read down the list. There was Ralph Waldo Emerson on the fourth floor. Bronson Alcott was working for Digital; so was Henry's enemy at *Dial* magazine, Margaret Fuller. They were all there, all the transcendentalists of Concord, having somehow skipped through time to sell their talents to Uncle Kenny. I was genuinely confused; too much sun, perhaps, too much immersion in the nineteenth century, too much contrast in one day.

"Conference rooms," someone said behind me. "We named them after the people around here. Homage to Concord."

It was Virgil, dressed in his cowboy clothes with his shoulder-length hair falling around his silver necklaces.

"Thank God you explained," I said. "I thought I was going mad."

We began on the first floor. He showed me the great computer brain, which I had already seen. We went to the second floor, where, in the central part of the building, I saw row upon row of cubicles stretching off into the distance, out of sight almost.

"This building is an innovation. All the cubicles are the same height here, regardless of rank," Virgil explained.

The real Virgil took his Dante deeper and deeper into the depths of hell. I was guided ever upward toward the light. But there really was not much to see — floor after floor of identical cubicles. I could see inside some of them as we passed down the labyrinth of hallways. People were hunched over their terminals, their backs to the doorway. Some had decorated their walls with vistas of American landscapes — the Rockies, deserts, waterfalls, and wild animals. Some cubicle walls were simply lined with shelves stacked with reports and computer manuals.

In time we came to Virgil's own cubicle, and here he demonstrated to me the uses of his computer. Since he was some species of manager, he had a larger, more powerful piece of equipment, which he attempted, and more or less failed, to describe to me. At one point he gave me a demonstration of the marvels of technology. He explained that he could communicate with anyone in the building through his terminal. After some fiddling with his keyboard, he typed in a message to a nearby colleague. There was no response. He tried another tack, then another. Finally, in exasperation, he stood up on his chair and shouted down the row of cubicles.

"Mike," he said. "Turn on your machine. You've got a message coming in."

Mike obeyed.

HELLO, MIKE, THIS IS A DEMO, Virgil typed.

Mike's computer, after a delay of a few seconds, slowly, letter by letter, responded.

HELLO, I READ YOU, O, K,

"You see," Virgil said. "You can communicate all through this building."

We moved on, passing through hallways and rooms. I asked to visit the conference room that was named for Henry Thoreau, and Virgil dutifully guided me there. It was an empty, windowless room with a long table, well insulated from the former pear orchard and the surrounding landscape Henry had once praised. On the wall hung a woodcut with a quote from Henry: "In wildness," it said, "is the preservation of the world."

We moved upward again and came to a vast interior room. Huge anacondalike wires ran across the ceiling, twisting and snaking downward to machines that sat on the floor in a dimmed, subdued light. Here, Virgil explained, was the essence of the building. Here the prototypes for the networking systems that would later be developed and sold were designed. There were only a few people in the room. It was past five o'clock, and the cubicles and halls were beginning to swarm with departing workers. But in one corner a group of diligent engineers stood puzzling around one machine. As Virgil explained, a "ghost" had appeared. Things were happening inside the machine that should not happen, and they were occurring not in an orderly fashion but in a seemingly random pattern.

"If it happens regularly you can fix it," Virgil said. "If it's random, it's trouble. They're worried. They might be here all night."

We left the worried engineers and ascended to the next floor. In one area was an electronic workshop of some sort, all cluttered with computers and snips of wires. We came to a cafeteria. Virgil took me to a walkway that led to what would soon be the second building of the complex and proudly showed me a large maple tree that had been left standing between the two buildings. It was actually quite a pleasant touch. The tree cast a green shade over the glassed-in walkway. Finally we reached the fifth and highest floor, where we wandered through the maze of cubicles and ended up on the western side of the building. We were at one of the highest points in the town, and the view was splendid. Below us the slope of the former pear orchard rolled away to the wide highway, which was crowding up at this hour with the cars of commuters. Beyond we could see the old fields of a former farm that was deserted when the highway came through, and beyond that I could see the low ridge on which my cottage was located. Somewhere over there the meadow would still be giving off the rich odor of fresh-cut hay, the indigo buntings would be calling, and the grasshoppers would be scrambling over the fallen grasses. I felt a pang of loneliness.

Beyond the ridge, beyond the stretching penaplain, deep blue now in the lowering afternoon sky, I saw Mount Wachusett — Henry Thoreau's lonely peak, standing apart, without society.

*

By June 21 I had been living in my cottage for one year. It rained that night, a warm, sustaining rain that dripped off the leaves in the hickory grove and filtered down through the tangle of wildflowers into the soil of the meadow. Just before going to bed I went out and stood in the open air, allowing the cleansing coolness of the sky to fall over my shoulders. I was alone, and below the meadow, in my old house, a light was burning, a brighter reflection of the warmer light of the oil lamps in my cottage. I thought of a flicker I had heard the night before. For some unknown reason, in the middle of the night, it had let out a long whinny from the woods beside the cottage. The sound woke me instantly, and I felt a strange sense of communion with the bird — a fellow traveler in the experiment of life, a spark in a generally lifeless and desolate universe. I felt a similar communion seeing the light below the meadow. I felt that I and my family, my friends and allies and acquaintances, were all shrinking down into the small, wild spaces of the world. I was determined now to stay on.

The rain slowed, spilled to a mere drip in the surrounding woods; a cricket started up, and deep in the mat of grasses on the south side of the meadow I saw the bright flash of a firefly.

Epilogue

EARLY THAT SUMMER I finished reading the journals of Henry Thoreau. I had already completed my father's and my brother's journals. Delving into these personal accounts of other lives made me think back on the time, one year earlier, when I had first moved into my cottage.

I originally built the cottage because my marriage was breaking up. I was broke, I didn't have a good place to live, and I was cut off from the most meaningful landscape I had ever come to know. I was at the end of my tether. But then so was Henry when he went to Walden. So was Megan Lewis after her husband died. So were Alice Dart, Emil and Minna, Bill the Green Man, and Prince Rudolph. It seemed that everybody I had concerned myself with that year had been through some sort of trial. Most had recovered and survived, and some, myself included, had gone on to experience small, private ecstasies.

Perhaps this account of that single year in my life is being set down too soon after it occurred for me to make any sense of it. The places you live, or the things that happen to you, or the people you take up with may seem accidental, but I believe that we are all reflections of one another, and that the people I knew that year, the experiences I had, and the landscape in which I lived were all in fact an extension of myself, an invented, imaginary world.

Yet the place was indeed real. In fact, I continued to live in the cottage for two more years. During that time there were very few changes on the ridge. I expanded the garden along the western wall. The grasses grew thicker in the meadow, and to the north and west the woodlands continued to flourish. If anything, the ridge seemed to grow wilder. But at some point I knew I would have to leave the cottage — if I had stayed on, life would have become normal there — and so, by the end of that first year, I had begun to think more seriously about building a "real" house on the land.

I had continued to admire the ideas of Henry Thoreau's contemporary Andrew Jackson Downing. I had even come across a reference to him — a derogatory one — in *Walden,* where Thoreau took Downing to task for recommending earth-colored houses. But in spite of this squabbling between my mentors, I was able to make a clear choice and decided to build a replica of one of Downing's cottages. The construction of that place — the various modifications and misadventures that are so much a part of house building — is another story entirely. Suffice it to say that after a year and a half of struggle, there was yet another Gothic Revival house beside the little meadow, this one properly constructed by a craftsman who, as fate would have it, was named Jackson. I moved into the place toward the end of a strangely snowless winter.

On my first night there it finally did snow, a beautiful slow drift that covered the winterkilled meadow, the stone walls, and the steep gables of my new house. Just as I was falling asleep I heard, coming from the woods beside my former cottage, the most lonesome, tragic howl I have ever known. The sound echoed through the pines. It reverberated along the stone walls and seemed to permeate the rooms of my as yet unfurnished house. The call was that of a lone coyote, and later that winter this single individual was joined by another. By spring a whole pack had taken up residence on the ridge.

In spite of the increasing wildness of the area, I was now once more living behind real walls. Even though I had a house with many tall, narrow windows opening onto gardens and terraces and parterres, I lived cut off from the outdoors, in the manner of most moderately well-off people in the Western world. Life there was luxurious. I had running hot water, heat, a proper stove, and a well-insulated dwelling that successfully kept the winter winds at bay. My children, who continued to come on a regular basis, had rooms of their own, and I settled into a generally civilized existence.

Often in spring, after the weather warmed, I would think back on my first year in the little cottage. That single year, which had been filled with so many new discoveries, had proved an excellent refinement of views I had been developing before I moved there. Day to day, my so-called primitive way of life had sharpened those things I already knew about myself: that I find great solace in living close to the cycles of the natural year, and that living in this way, I feel more in touch with deeper, less evident cycles in the universe, closer to the moving spirit of the land. More to the point, I discovered firsthand, as Henry Thoreau so often taught, that the essence of civilization is not the multiplication of wants but the elimination of need. In our time it never hurts to rediscover such simple truths for oneself.